MASQUES

Stefany Anne Golberg

Published April 15, 2015
Fallen Bros. Press
29403 N Enrose Ave.
Rancho Palos Verdes CA 90275

ISBN-13: 978-0692427835

Original Publication:

From **The Smart Set**: *Everything is Leaf*, April 23, 2014; *The Ghost of Anne Frank,* October 20, 2009; *Eng and Chang*, April 27, 2011; *The Tragic Sense of Life*, December 6, 2013; *The Berlin Wall*, November 10, 2014; *Martha*, September 17, 2014; *Devil's Dictionary*, September 26, 2011; *Godot*, January 14, 2013; *Mad Meg*, May 3, 2012; *Moravia*, July 25, 2013; *Happy New Year*, December 23, 2013; *A Life in Letters*, January 18, 2012; *Kings*, August 26, 2010; *Apocalypse*, January 21, 2014

From **New England Review**: *Marat/Sade in Las Vegas*, September 4, 2014

From **Spolia**: *Boredom*, July 3013; *Hysteria*, November 2013

From **3 Quarks Daily**: *Two Weeks in China*, December 08, 2008; *Waiting*, October 31, 2011

For Morgan

Death Mask, Museum of Gold, Bogota, Columbia. Photo © Vincent T. Meis

Contents **Page**

1. Everything Is Leaf.. 1

2. The Ghost of Anne Frank 5

3. Marat and Sade in Las Vegas........................ 11

4. Eng and Chang... 15

5. The Tragic Sense of Life 23

6. The Berlin Wall 35

7. Martha 45

8. Boredom... 53

9. The Prairie 61

10. Devil's Dictionary.................................... 69

11. Godot... 83

12. Mad Meg.. 95

13. Two Weeks in China................................. 105

14. Hysteria 129

15. Moravia 137

16. Happy New Year....................................... 145

17. Waiting.. 155

18. A Life in Letters....................................... 165

19. Kings 175

20. Apocalypse... 185

Internet Photo (unattributed)

Everything Is Leaf

Gloom rains down during early April days in the north. The sky is heavy and stuffed with shadows. A goldfinch at the bird feeder looks ridiculous; his molting winter feathers are a wreck. Everything about his half-golden face says hope, the uncombed horror of hope. This is the time we look for anything that reminds us of life. These are the days of stick-seeking and leaf-hunting, of changing our eyes into microscopes. On the windowsill, a slug! under a pile of leaves, an infinitesimal green something. Eliot was so right about April and its cruelty.

***

Found among the notes of the poet Johann Wolfgang Goethe is a stupendous claim: Everything is leaf. This statement seems too beautiful to be science. Goethe came to this idea on a trip to Italy in the late 1700s. The more Goethe looked at plants, and lived and breathed with plants, the more profoundly he felt poetry's limits. He turned to botany and began publishing scientific works. He created his own study of seeing, which he called "morphology." Goethe's love of plants followed the same path that all lasting love must take. Goethe wanted to know plants from their most essential beginnings, wanted to touch their seeds, follow their cycles. He couldn't be satisfied just wandering around parks, glancing at the flowers and pronouncing metaphors upon them—Goethe had to understand what a plant truly is. Everything is leaf, he discovered at last, every part of a plant is leaf. The cotyledon, the foliage, the cataphylls, the petals—a plant is fundamentally leaf. Goethe published this intimate memoir of his relationship with leaves and named it *The Metamorphosis of Plants*.

It's natural that Goethe stumbled upon the everything-ness of leaf while wandering the lush countryside of Naples. Could he could have had his realization trudging through the barren, early spring gardens of Weimar? "The Neapolitan firmly believes that he lives in Paradise and takes a very dismal view of northern countries," Goethe wrote in his notebook. "*Sempre neve, case di legno, gran ignoranza, ma denari assai*—that is how he pictures our lives. For the edification of all northerners, this means: 'Snow all the year round, wooden houses, great ignorance, but lots of money.'" That is to say, a leaf in Germany is a mostly invisible thing. It is an entr'acte, a promise. In the northern parts of the world, the leaves hide inside the sticks; the sticks, for most of the year, look dead. And only a poet or a flimflammer could come up with the notion that something hardly visible is everything.

The more closely Goethe researched plants, the further they retreated. Every open door led to a room of doors that were locked. But Goethe was accepting. This, he wrote in *Indecision and Surrender* (1818), is the very nature of intuition, observation, and contemplation, Research leads us closer to mystery. Between experience and ideas is a chasm, and all our efforts to bridge this gap are in vain. Still, Goethe wrote, we keep on trying. "We strive eternally to overcome this hiatus with reason, intellect, imagination, faith, emotion, illusion, or—if we are capable of nothing better—with folly… we justifiably take flight into poetry, giving by way of change a new form to an old song." Science made the unfathomability of plants visible to Goethe; poetry made his experience of plants boundless.

Nature is everything, Goethe wrote, just as everything is leaf. "We live within her, yet are foreign to her. Conversing with us endlessly, she never divulges her secret… Nature is even the unnatural. Those who cannot see her everywhere do not see her clearly anywhere." Nature isn't just the stuff in the cracks of the concrete that holds the Empire State building up to the sky. Concrete is made from the stuff of nature, just as fire escapes in Harlem are reflections of Nature's designs. So you see, Nature is everywhere, just like Goethe said. And yet Nature, being everywhere, is hidden. We color the voids with poetry, and knowledge, especially in the early days of April, when the leaves keep themselves so hidden we think we might never see them again.

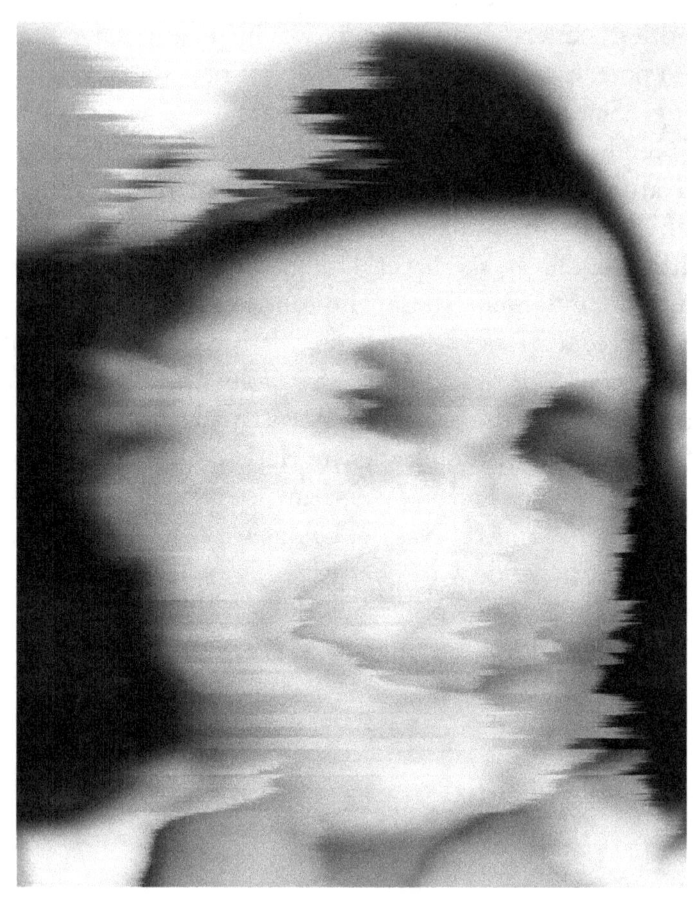

Anne Frank (altered photo), 1944

The Ghost of Anne Frank

I can't stop watching the film clip of Anne Frank. Ever since the Anne Frank House museum posted it on their new Anne Frank YouTube channel, I have watched it again and again. I must have watched it a hundred times. It is 20 seconds of shaky, black-and-white silence, in which Anne Frank appears at a window on a summer day in 1941. It is the only known film of Anne Frank.

Only, it's not a film of Anne Frank. At least not intentionally. The stars of the film are a newlywed couple, walking out of the house next door. The bride carries a huge bouquet of flowers and wears a modest skirt suit. She holds the arm of a lanky groom, who dons a top hat and tails. They are happy. The street gathers to watch them, the windows in the surrounding buildings fill with onlookers.

The film's guest star is Merwedeplein, the street in Amsterdam where the Frank family lived before they went into hiding the following summer at 263 Prinsengracht—now known as the Secret Annex. It's a clear day on Merwedeplein and everything seems as it should: girls hold their mothers' hands, teenage boys ride bicycles, cars whiz past a nearby park. It's a time when the Jews of Holland were only being deported in handfuls; there's no sign at all of a country living under occupation.

Ten seconds into the film, the camera pans up from the newlyweds and the street to a girl sticking her head out a second floor window. Watching the 20-second clip, there's no reason to notice this girl. Except that the girl is Anne Frank. And so, knowing that you will see her, and then seeing her, you cannot concentrate on anything else in the film. Her animated head bobs around, excited, watching the couple, then the street, then the couple again, then the women in the window next door, then back over her shoulder to someone behind her, then the couple, the street again, women again—all in five seconds. She would love to follow the married couple, run after them down the street. Mundane burdens—homework, an unfinished lunch—keep her inside, the burdens of a 12-year-old girl.

The more you watch the clip, the more you see only Anne Frank, even in the 15 seconds when she's absent. Everything happening in the center of the frame is haunted by one peripheral moment of … wait, there's Anne Frank, is it really—there she…! She's gone. The clip stops, and you watch it again. Twenty seconds of impressionistic filler starring a window and a ghost in the shape of a girl.

It's funny how ghosts always appear at windows. They're always peeking out, or trying to get in, or—seen from outside wandering back and forth—floating in and out of the window's frame. Think Catherine in *Wuthering Heights*, Peter Quint in *Turn of the Screw*, the charming maiden in *The Deserted House*, Poe's *The Haunted Palace*…the list is long. Nothing represents longing and loss like a window, especially a haunted one. The word "haunt" has its roots in the word "home." Ghosts are always trying to find their way home, or find themselves lost in a home where they are unwanted. Even when they are in a home, they never feel "at home." Ghosts are permanently homeless. They live in the space between inside and outside, between home and not home, like a window. Lurking about a window, the ghost hopes to see and be seen, aching to be free. Anne Frank probably spent many hours at the window of Merwedeplein 37, caught in the limbo between being a 12-year-old girl who must stay at home and a dreamer, a natural flâneur forced to wander the streets of Amsterdam in her imagination.

During two years of her short life, Anne Frank would spend much of her time haunting the attic window of the Secret Annex. In *Diary of a Young Girl*, windows show up again and again as symbols of love, fear, and independence, sometimes all at once.

> One night during the Pentecost holiday, for instance, when it was so hot, I struggled to keep my eyes open until 11:30 so I could get a good look at the moon, all on my own for once. Alas, my sacrifice was in vain, since there was too much glare and I couldn't risk opening a window. Another time, several months ago, I happened to be upstairs one night when the window was open. I didn't go back down until it had to be closed again. The dark, rainy evening, the wind, the racing clouds, had me spellbound; it was the first time in a year and a half that I'd seen the night face-to-face. After that evening my longing to see it again was even greater than my fear of burglars, a dark rat-infested house, or robberies. I went downstairs all by myself and looked out the windows in the kitchen and private office.

Windows also came to mean a loss of innocence for Anne Frank. Like Peter Pan and the Lady of Shalott, what awaits Anne Frank outside the window is the horrible freedom of experience and understanding. "I saw two Jews through the curtains yesterday, it was a horrible feeling, just as if I had betrayed them and was now watching them in their misery." By the window, Anne Frank sees the arrests, listens to the bombings. She bears witness to the crimes on the street she cannot access, and, by watching, is implicated in them. Yet, from the street perspective, as Anne sits unseen, watching from behind the window, imprisoned, she is the flipside of that same crime. The window is both protection and prison.

There's one more Anne Frank video clip with a haunted window. It shows 44 seconds of the famous chestnut tree outside the Secret Annex window. The tree is captured from all angles, starting from the outside, with the Annex window in the background. It is the vantage Anne Frank herself would only see once. In the video, the tree looks healthy and dappled with sun. A breeze makes it dance a bit and you can hear distant sounds of the Amsterdam street: birdsong, the tolling of church bells, the rushing of the Prinsengracht canal, the breeze again. Of course, the tree would have been silent for Anne Frank, as the families in the attic were rarely allowed to open the window. In an old black-and-white photograph of the attic on the *Anne Frank House* website, the chestnut tree is a ghost in the background, bare limbs hunched in the distance. The caption of this photo reads: "It is dark and damp and there are rats."

For all the gumption and personality apparent in her writing, and apparent again in the five seconds of film in which Anne Frank exists as a moving image—I can't ever picture Anne Frank on the street, taking a stroll, playing. I'll always picture her half indoors and half out, neither here nor there, with only her imagination to connect her to everyday experience.

> This morning, when I was sitting in front of the window and taking a long, deep look outside at God and nature, I was happy, just plain happy.... Whenever you're feeling lonely or sad, try going to the loft on a beautiful day and looking outside. Not at the houses and the rooftops, but at the sky. As long as you can look fearlessly at the sky, you'll know that you're pure within and will find happiness once more.

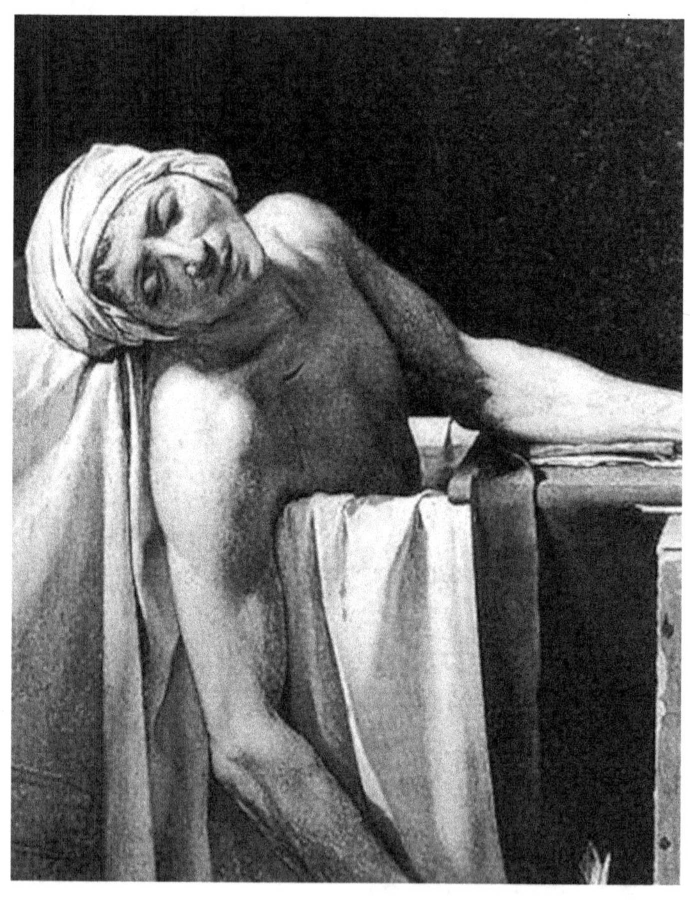

Marat (from production poster)

Marat and Sade in Las Vegas

In the days before personal computers, when Xeroxing books was a punishable crime, I hand-typed the entirety of T*he Persecution and Assassination of Jean-Paul Marat as Performed by the Inmates of the Asylum of Charenton Under the Direction of the Marquis de Sade* for my personal collection, as such a book was not generally available in 1980s Las Vegas. I'd borrowed a copy from the UNLV library. *Marat/Sade* is a play written by the German postwar playwright Peter Weiss. Weiss incorporates a play within the play, one written by de Sade, to be performed by his fellow inmates at the Charenton asylum. So Weiss's actors play lunatics staging de Sade's play, and also act as various historical figures with whom de Sade has philosophical dialogues.

What was the appeal, for a fifteen-year-old girl, of a story about a nihilistic and lecherous Revolution-era Frenchman—portrayed by a postwar German avant-gardist—who writes and directs a play in an insane asylum? In *Marat/ Sade*, an actress plays a somnambulist who plays the part of Charlotte Corday, assassin of the Jacobin leader Jean-Paul Marat, as he lay in the bathtub. Marat is played by a paranoid schizophrenic. The radical priest Jacques Roux, who stabbed himself to death in prison, is played by an inmate in a straightjacket. These characters felt very true to me, their concerns urgent ones. They screamed for freedom, and for justice, and then broke into ecstatic singing, and laughed until the asylum staff beat them back into the corners.

The passage that affected me most was a conversation between the Marquis de Sade and Jean-Paul Marat on the nature of life and death. Peter Weiss wrote this dialogue between the two historical figures—who had never met in real life—as a playing-out of the psychological motivations behind the French Revolution, about which I knew very little at that time.

MARAT:
I read in your books de Sade
in one of your immortal works
that the basis of all life is death

SADE:
Correct, Marat
But man has given a false importance to death
Any animal plant or man who dies
adds to Nature's compost heap
becomes the manure without which
nothing could grow nothing could be created
Death is simply part of the process
Every death even the cruelest death
drowns in the total indifference of Nature . . .

The Marquis goes on like that, and Marat counters:

Against Nature's silence I use action

In the vast indifference I invent a meaning
I don't watch unmoved I intervene
and say that this and this are wrong
and I work to alter them and improve them . . .

It was always important to intervene and say this and this are wrong—Marat's argument here was solid. I couldn't understand what he meant, though, about inventing meaning against nature's silence. Meaning was not something you could paste onto death. It was like the Marquis de Sade said, death was important only insofar as it made way for new life, and nature didn't care about either.

I hadn't really thought about nature until then—I lived in Las Vegas and didn't think deserts counted as nature. Though often I would stand in my backyard at night and look up at the stars. They were indifferent to me. The vast treeless sand-scape of Vegas, the mountains that dwarfed the casinos in the valley—all unmoved by my small, individual experience. Surely, it mattered little to the stars or trees whether I lived or died. The house next door looked as calm as it ever did, even though my friend Mark had died only the year before. I eventually decided that the Marquis de Sade also meant human nature, because he realized that the heart of man was apathetic and all acts of kindness manipulation and façade.

I spent a year's worth of evenings in my father's office typing up *Marat/Sade*. I did not know how to type properly and did not intend to learn. I typed and retyped the words until I had a complete manuscript. I had never been so close to anything in my life as I became to that text. I learned its message letter by letter, and when I was finished, I never read the play again.

Eng & Chang (photogtaph) circa 1870

Eng and Chang

It's still a question, whether Eng had to die that night. They had an agreement, he and Chang, and theirs was a bond that would not break easily. They were linked physically from birth; they depended on each other come what may. If Chang drank, Eng got drunk. If Chang loved, Eng found love too. When Chang suffered a stroke that left the otherwise healthy Eng dragging about an invalid, doom was in the air. No one was sure how the cards would play out, but they both knew the backup plan. Not long before, during one of Chang's frequent drunken rages, he pointed a knife at his dear brother and promised, "I'm going to cut your gut out!" after which Eng pulled Chang to the doctor and insisted they be cut apart at once. The doctor refused, but assured the twins he would perform an emergency operation when one twin died. So, for Eng, the January night in 1874 when Chang lay finally dead beside him was the denouement to the unresolved dilemma of his life. After years of suffering Chang's drunks, after the détentes, the compromises, the promises—that January night, Eng knew that if he weren't divorced immediately from Chang, he too would die. "Then I am going," Eng told his family.

And go he did.

We can't think of Chang and Eng Bunker as separate any more than they could. These were the original twins from Siam after all who gave conjoined twins their euphemism. We can't think of them apart, but neither can we think of them as one without being seized with dread. We think, no way in hell could I have lived my life that way. Perhaps we would have chosen early death. Suffice it to say, a life in which the most basic bodily functions are shared—walking, defecating, having sex with your wife—is so inconceivable to the unjoined person, one might as well imagine living in a two-dimensional universe. It seems impossible that Eng and Chang Bunker managed to construct real lives out of their impossible situation. That each brother would fall in love, and marry. That, between them, they would father 21 children, run separate households, become gentlemen farmers. That they had distinct personalities, distinct interests and cares and still carried on as one. And so, because they lived and thrived, the remarkable tale of the Siamese twins gets told again and again.

Chang and Eng underwent countless medical examinations to figure out just how connected they were. Most doctors came up with the same conclusion: if they separated, Chang and Eng would likely have died. It was also possible that separation might leave one survivor. This last possibility was unthinkable for the Bunker brothers. Theirs was a life shared, independent but together, and that was that. To separate would have meant completely rethinking that life. To separate, Eng and Chang Bunker would have had to believe that the only thing holding them together was some cartilage and skin at the torso. Skin, and two complete livers that were fused. (One can visit this esteemed double liver at the Mütter Museum in Philadelphia). Some say Eng died of fright, but who can say what scared him most? Death, surely. Maybe Eng thought he would be lonely without Chang, or feared the operation that would remove his dead brother from him like a bunion. But maybe he feared that, even if he survived, he would not be Eng without Chang.

In the presence of twins we lose our mental footing. How is it that two people can exist from what was to be a single person? It's not without reason that twins are characters in our mythologies and our horror stories: Castor and Pollux, the Mayan Hero Twins of the Popol Vuh, Romulus and Remus, Lava and Kusha, the little girls in "The Shining". Twins are a symbolic externalization of what we have decided is our dualistic nature. One twin is always good, one is bad. One is beautiful and the other ugly. One is mortal, the other divine. One is destruction and the other creation. Even so, twins are always a team. They may be in conflict, but the goodness of the good twin is inextricable from the evil of the evil twin. How often is it that twins are more familiar to us by their "collective" name: the Gemini, the Ashvins? The tales of twins are there to remind us how good and evil both reside inside us, impossibly scrambled—not to mention (more often than not) beyond our control, and that we humans are just the breakfast plates upon which our scrambled values are served.

And if we are made tipsy by the sight of twins, the sight of conjoined twins bowls us over. We look at Chang and Eng—at all conjoined twins—and think, no, it cannot be that way. There they are, two human beings sharing a heart, a leg, a head! We think of monsters, deformity, and the terrifying chaos of Nature's whim. Twins make us question what is right and natural for an autonomous, individual human being. Conjoined twins make us afraid for a reason far deeper and far more personal: they make us question our very status as autonomous, individual human beings. For as much as we debate what constitutes a good body or a functional body or a defective body, we all agree on this: Our body must be our own, it must belong only to us. When we look at Chang and Eng, we wonder, at what point could our own individuality dissolve into another's? If we shared an arm? A leg? A brain? A heart? A life?

We take it for granted, then, that Siamese twins would separate if they could choose, especially now that 21st century medical advances make it possible. In a 2000 BBC documentary, South African surgeon Heinz Röde—a leading specialist in the division of conjoined twins—summed up the condition as such: "My own philosophy," he said, "is that twins are born to be separated." Which is to say, Röde believes people are born to be separate. In separating conjoined twins, we feel that we are saying to them, "You have a right to be alone, to be individuals alone, in your own body alone, determining your own destiny, alone." This is the very definition of a free self, the knowledge that you can always extract yourself from another. Yet, if you ask conjoined twins, most seem quite comfortable with their shared bond. "We'd never agree to an operation," Dasha Krivoshlyapova told the BBC. "We just don't need it." "Even when we were little we didn't want one," said Masha Krivoshlyapova. "We are a little collective."

This last sentiment is simultaneously adorable and horrifying. For what would it mean to turn our lives into a "little collective," to permanently, inextricably attach our fate to another's, always experience our lives in terms of another?

Would it not make us unsure where our own "self" began and ended, unsure that we were the tellers of our own jokes, the designers of our own hopes, the caretakers of our own needs? How could we accept thinking of "me" as "us", accept being unfree? In other words, what we see, and fear in Chang and Eng is love.

In 2006, conjoined twins Abby and Brittany Hensel decided to share their 16th birthdays with the world in a special for The Learning Channel. Far more dramatic in appearance than Chang and Eng, Abby and Brittany look like one grand body with two heads. Their well-coordinated walk is something of an acrobatic miracle. In the documentary, the mother of these blond, cheery, all-American twins describes encountering her daughters' recent exploration of their body/bodies. She found them one day, she says, running their hands over each other's flesh, trying to find out how their bodies worked together, asking, Do you feel that? Do you feel that? Do you feel that? This delicate, awkward manipulating struck me as a very 16-year-old endeavor. Unlike the solitary childhood discovery of the body, where everything is fresh and strange, the teenage version is a re-imagining of the flesh, done in the company of another. The thrill of fingers running over arms and legs, the wondering whose body is whose, which parts of your body belong to you, which feel more complete when given over. Do you feel that? Do you feel that? Do you feel that? It is experiencing the line of demarcation between my pleasure and yours as a hazy border drawn in sand. "The telescopic sensation of coming into contact with the cellular infinity of another body's existence," as Joseph Brodsky wrote. It is the realization that the qualities we think of as uniquely ours, perhaps our best qualities, might be shaped with the hands of another, and go spiraling toward infinity with every touch.

The last thing Eng did in his final hour was to put his arms around Chang. I've read that, in his shocked state, he asked once or twice for Chang to be moved closer to him. It's not clear whether his request was met, or how Chang could have been much closer.

Miguel de Unamuno by Ramon Casas

The Tragic Sense of Life

Miguel de Unamuno's earliest memory was of a bomb landing on the roof of his neighbor's house during Spain's final Carlist War. The philosopher and poet was born in conflict. Unamuno was a Spanish patriot and one of its most outspoken critics; a Basque who was also a Spaniard; a child who wanted to be a Catholic saint; a philosopher who was suspicious of philosophy.

Miguel de Unamuno woke one night in 1897, tormented by dreams of falling into nothingness. Just a few months earlier, Unamuno's infant son Raimundo had contracted meningitis. Raimundo's illness disabled him physically and mentally. He was not expected to live long. Miguel de Unamuno believed that this tragedy was his fault, divine punishment for turning away from his childhood faith and embracing scientific rationalism. That night in 1897, Unamuno's wife Concha found her husband sobbing. She held him and called out, "My child!" Years later, Unamuno wrote of this experience and the lasting effect of those two words.

In a moment of supreme, of abysmal anguish,

> wracked with superhuman weeping, when she saw me in the claws of the Angel of Nothingness, she cried out to me from the depths of her maternal being, superhuman and divine: "My child!" I discovered then all that God had done for me in this woman, the mother of my children, my own virgin mother...my mirror of holy, divine unconsciousness and eternity.

This "crisis of 1897" marked the crossroad of Miguel de Unamuno's spiritual and intellectual journey. The philosopher would build no system that would eliminate his inner turmoil. He would not turn his back on the Angel of Nothingness. Rather, he would embrace this angel as his wife had embraced him in his grief. Miguel de Unamuno would develop from his nightmare a messy, passionate philosophy of conflict, a philosophy of tragedy. In short, a philosophy of himself.

***

In 1913, Miguel de Unamuno published a book called *The Tragic Sense of Life*. It was considered—in his time—to be a masterpiece, an influential work of early existentialist philosophy. But *The Tragic Sense of Life* is more (or you might say less) than a work of philosophy. It is a deeply personal account of one man's anguish in the night.

The book begins with an answer:

"I am a man; no other man do I deem a stranger."

The questions are the questions we have asked since the dawn of consciousness: Who am I? To what end do I exist? "I," answered Unamuno, "am a man." Man—the individual human life—was the beginning of everything for Unamuno. "The man of flesh and bone; the man who is born, suffers, and dies—above all, who dies; the man who eats and drinks and plays and sleeps and thinks and wills; the man who is seen and heard; the brother, the real brother." This man was not be confused with that other kind of "man"—the *homo sapiens* of Linneaus, or Aristotle's featherless biped, or the social contractor of Rousseau. This other kind of "man" is not a man at all. It is the idea of a man. This man has no sex, no country, no nightmares—this man is an abstraction. No, it was the real man of flesh and bone who concerned Unamuno. "I am a man" is the answer and it is also the question. Man, wrote Unamuno, is "at once the subject and supreme object of all philosophy, whether certain self-styled philosophers like it or not." Man, and not ideas. After all, philosophers too are made of flesh and bone, Unamuno reminded us, whether they like it or not.

We think that the task of philosophy, of science, of life, is to ask, "Why?" from some objective faraway place. But "why", writes Unamuno, only makes sense in view of "wherefore". Not just "why" but for what purpose? Not merely the cause of life but the end. Man possesses consciousness. But knowing is one thing, writes Unamuno, and living another. It is a mistake to think that just because people possess consciousness, ideas alone make the man. Philosophy, science, industry, morality—"we have filled the world with industrial marvels, with great factories, with roads, museums and libraries" and still we must ask: Was man made for ideas or were we made to serve the products of ideas? *Cogito ergo sum*, Descartes concluded—"I think" affirms my existence. But where in this statement, Unamuno wanted to know, was the real man behind the philosophy? Where was the René Descartes who loved poetry and mathematics, who desired heaven?

Closer to the truth, wrote Unamuno, is *sum, ergo cogito* —"I am, therefore I think." And yet, why not say, "I feel, therefore I am"? Or "I will, therefore I am?" We are thinking beings, to be sure, but we also have joy and we suffer. We think with our whole spirit and body. We feel in our bodies and our minds.

> Man is said to be a reasoning animal. I do not know why he has not been defined as an affective or feeling animal.Perhaps that which differentiates him from other animals is feeling rather than reason. More often I have seen a cat reason than laugh or weep. Perhaps it weeps or laughs inwardly—but then perhaps, also inwardly, the crab resolves equations of the second degree.

"I am," wrote Unamuno, "But who am I? All we have is our individuality" wrote Unamuno—if we are something else we are nothing. "They tell me I am here to realize I know not what social end; but I feel that I, like each one of my fellows, am here to realize myself, to live." All I have is myself, wrote Unamuno—and still he tried to run away. Consciousness, Unamuno learned, was not all it was cracked up to be. Consciousness, which has shown us many interesting truths about existence, has brought even more confusion. The more systems of thought we develop —the more equations we prove—the more contradictions we are handed. The more we learn about life on Earth, the more mysterious the universe becomes. When we back away from this confusion, we become hypocrites, wrote Unamuno. Yet, when we confront the chaos, we suffer.

Consciousness is our gift and our enemy. "Consciousness", wrote Unamuno, "is a disease."

This thing called consciousness, we learn, is simply awareness of one's own limitations. More specifically, it is consciousness of death. And this is the tragic sense of life.

Marcus Aurelius, St. Augustine, Pascal, Rousseau, Rene, Obermann, Thomson, Leopardi, Vigny, Lenau, Kleist, Amiel, Quental, Kierkegaard—these are just a few men of flesh and bone who had a bad case of the disease, wrote Unamuno, men "burdened with wisdom rather than with knowledge." These diseased men are Unamuno's kindred spirits, men for whom the tragic was a constant companion. They are individuals who chose to embrace the great horrible Doubt that lurks at the heart of modern existence rather than profess a cure. "It is not enough," wrote Unamuno, "to cure the plague; we must learn to weep for it."

It all sounds a little morbid, Unamuno admitted. But it is nearly always through disease that we pay attention to our health. (And whoever proved, asked Unamuno, that man is either healthy or cheerful by nature?) From the darkness of anguish we emerge into the light, like when Dante came up from the depths of Hell to see the stars again. It is precisely through the disease of consciousness, the conflict and tragedy of life, that Miguel de Unamuno was able to find his soul. And this, for Unamuno, was worth a million good ideas.

"A misere sung in common by a multitude tormented by destiny," he wrote, "has as much value as a philosophy."

***

Imagine yourself in a small boat that has stopped midway between a river and a raging waterfall below. This is how the person with the tragic sense of life lives. It is how Miguel de Unamuno lived—in a state of existential crisis, hovering over the abyss.

Imagine, now, that you are dead. You can't do it; no matter how hard you try. It is literally impossible, wrote Unamuno, to imagine ourselves as not existing, no matter how great our imagination. Sit for a moment, he suggested, and try to imagine your mind—your consciousness—as it is when you are in a deep, dreamless sleep. It makes your head hurt. Try even harder and you will start to feel crazy. "It is like a cramped cell," wrote Unamuno, "against the bars of which my soul beats its wings in vain. Its lack of air stifles me. More, more, and always more!"

> I want to be myself, and yet without ceasing to be myself to be others as well, to merge myself into the totality of things visible and invisible, to extend myself into the illimitable of space and to prolong myself into the infinite of time. Not to be all and for ever is as if not to be—at least, let me be my whole self, and be so for ever and ever. And to be the whole of myself is to be everybody else. Either all or nothing!

Existence is the longing to live—to live and live and live. And yet, consciousness is the knowledge that we will die. We are, as Martin Heidegger wrote (himself influenced by Unamuno), Beings-toward-Death. But to be supremely aware of our mortality is to hunger for immortality. We want to live and yet live forever. The whole thing is a contradiction.

"Contradiction?" wrote Unamuno. "To be sure! … Of

course there is contradiction! … Contradiction! Of course! Since we only live in and by contradictions, since life is tragedy and the tragedy is perpetual struggle, without victory or the hope of victory, life is contradiction." This surrender to contradiction, for Unamuno, is what it means to be a man, to live as a whole man. We affirm life as we question it, and question the more we affirm. For Unamuno, exclamation points and question marks are the same. There ought to be an entirely new punctuation mark called an "unamuno" to express passionate, affirmative doubt.

"Eternity, eternity!—that is the supreme desire!" But why? Isn't it this hunger for immortality that stifles our enjoyment of life? Isn't it the "frenzied love of life" that most often urges us to long for death? asked Unamuno. If we are to die, why shouldn't we all just die as soon as possible and for good, so that no more doomed consciousnesses tormented by their own mortality may come into being? What is the good of living?

Unamuno, of course, had no answer. We want live because we are alive. We want to live because we love life. There is a kinship between love and life and so there is a kinship between love and death. The more we surrender ourselves to all of life and all of death—the tragedy and joy, the confusion and clarity—the more we love. And love is our consolation.

***

One night in 1897, the poet and philosopher Miguel de Unamuno woke up sobbing, suffering with love for his son. And then Unamuno's wife, his childhood sweetheart, came to him, and put her arms around him and said, "My child!"

because she was suffering too. Unamuno found in his wife that night a little bit of something divine he had given up on years ago. She was his mirror, and he was hers, and together they dodged the Angel of Nothingness.

We are taught, "Love thy neighbor as thyself," wrote Unamuno, but this assumes we love our self. And if we have no sense of our own self, our own suffering, our own individuality, how can we love another? We are taught, "Love thy neighbor as thyself," but we are not even sure that we know what love is—is it sacrifice to home or country or to one's work or children? We are told "Live for the True, the Good, the Beautiful!" wrote Unamuno, but what is more vain and insincere? I love my neighbor, wrote Unamuno, not because he is good or beautiful, nor because I have sacrificed myself for him, but "because he lives in me and is part of my consciousness, because he is like me, because he is mine."

"I am a man," wrote Miguel de Unamuno, a man concerned only with his own life. Egotistical? asked Unamuno. Maybe. But we can only know Humanity, thought Unamuno, by knowing the one human being completely available to us—our self. Thus, the more I concern myself with my own life, the more I unite my pitiful, moving-toward-death self with all creation—with men and women and cats and crabs and yes, God too. The more I embrace my mortality, in other words, the more I become, essentially, eternal. "The thirst of eternity," writes Unamuno "is what is called love among men, and whosoever loves another wishes to eternalize himself in him." Contradiction? Yes!

"Love thy neighbor" was not mere theory for Unamuno. Unamuno's Spain was a country almost perpetually at war.

As rector of the University of Salamanca, Unamuno had quite a comfortable hideout in which to write his poems and plays. Yet he made this position a platform to speak out against fascism. Unamuno was removed from his post as rector in 1901 and forced into exile until the 1930s by the Rivera dictatorship for publicly opposing the regime. In 1936, when the Spanish Civil War broke out, Unamuno was again removed from his post as rector (and practically lynched) by Franco's Falangists. He died of a broken heart ten weeks later.

You can hear the strains of the Upanishads as much as the Gospels in *The Tragic Sense of Life*. Miguel de Unamuno was an Existentialist pantheist and a Catholic heretic and a Kierkegaardian mystic in one. (Indeed, Unamuno, learned Danish to read the then-mostly-unknown philosopher in the original, read American literature at a time when it was considered unserious by European intellectuals, taught himself fourteen languages to bring himself closer to the words of others because he loved other writers too.)

"I am a man," Miguel de Unamuno began his book, "no other man do I deem a stranger."

***

In Salamanca a hundred years ago, the beloved Miguel de Unamuno could be seen in the afternoon, drinking his coffee and folding *pajaritas*, little paper birds. Unamuno was an enthusiastic and celebrated paper folder—he wrote a mock "scientific" treatise on paper folding and origami shows up in a number of his novels and poems. A famous caricature of Unamuno shows him as part man and part *pajarita*. The tragic writer had a whimsical side—Unamuno was, paradoxically, an optimistic man. "Whosoever does not suffer does not enjoy," Unamuno might have said to you if you joined him at the café, "just as whosoever is insensible to cold is insensible to heat." Unamuno once considered writing a companion to The Tragic Sense of Life that would investigate the comic sense of life.

The man that most represented Unamuno's sense of optimistic skepticism was Don Quixote. Quixote's philosophy, he wrote, "can hardly be called idealism, since he did not fight for ideas; it was spiritualism, for he fought for the spirit." And what was the philosophy of Miguel de Unamuno? The self-proclaimed 'ideoclast'? Perhaps it can be found in a story recorded long ago by his friend Eduardo Ortega y Gasset. One day, while living in exile in France, Unamuno sat folding a menagerie in his garden. A boy wandered into the garden and was astonished by the paper animals. The boy turned to Unamuno and asked, "Don Miguel, do the little paper birds speak?" Unamuno was moved by the question. All at once, the paper birds became illuminated. One might call *The Tragic Sense of Life* a philosophy of little paper birds. A paper bird is a contradiction; it is sublime as it is simple. A paper bird is tragic; it is light but cannot fly. A paper bird is a protest against the injustice of a blank sheet of paper. And it is made of paper too.

Berlin Wall © Guy Le Querrec, 1989

The Berlin Wall

In the beginning, the Wall was made of barbed wire and soldiers. On some streets, cinder blocks had been stacked. In the Neukölln borough, on Harzer Straße, the Wall was about neck-high. East and West Berliners could look at each other over the Wall but they were not allowed to touch. In a photograph taken on the first day, August 13, 1961, two mothers stand on either side of a coil of wire that reaches to their knees. The babies they hold stretch out to each other, inches of air between their fingers. There seems to be a magnetic repulsion preventing them from holding hands. In another picture from that day, a young man in a crowd stands across from two border guards; a chest-high stack of cement is separating them. The young man appears to be asking one guard a question—both lay their hands on the Wall. Their hands are almost touching. The second guard smiles and leans upon the Wall as if he were socializing at a pub.

We will build the Wall in summer, declared GDR leader Walter Ulbricht, a summer day will be best. A Sunday in summer, when Berliners will be on holiday, having picnics at the lake. We will begin quietly, at night, when Berliners are sleeping, and work mostly in the dark. We will tear up the roads to make them impassable, and seal the border crossings. Railway lines will be cut off and train stations will be turned into deserts. Never again will East Berliners be able to leave of their own accord. And when the people of Berlin arise in the morning, our work will be complete.

To build a wall in the middle of a city, you must treat homes as highways. Front doors become backdoors. Windows become barricades. Rooms must be emptied of the evidence of people. The apartment buildings on Bernauer Straße began evacuating their people as soon as the Wall went up. In time they became vacant, apartment facades, creating an optical illusion of a city. In a few spots, apartments were completely absorbed into the body of the Berlin Wall. Before the Wall, a person in the East could just walk out the front door and enter West Berlin. After the Wall, front doors were nailed shut or walled up—so people went upstairs. They jumped to West Berlin from second- and third-story windows. In time, these were bricked over too.

The official name of the Berlin Wall, given by the East German authorities, was *Antifaschistischer Schutzwall*—"Anti-Fascist Protection Rampart." The insinuation was that their West German neighbors still had a long way to go toward de-Nazification. The Wall, claimed East German authorities, would protect East Germans from these Western fascists, who conspired to prevent the "will of the people" from building their socialist state. In English, it is a small grammatical difference between 'will' and 'wall'.

***

From the inside, the Wall was not a wall but a multiplicity of walls. The first wall made a hundred-mile band around the entirety of West Berlin. It ran through fields and rivers and blasted through city streets. This wall looked like what we think of when we think of the word 'wall'. On the Western side, the first wall was decorated with graffiti and slogans. West Germans and foreign tourists would come to this wall with binoculars and cameras. East Germans were unable to approach the first wall, as a heavily guarded three-mile-wide restricted zone surrounded it. On the Eastern side, this wall was kept plain. In the West, the first wall was the wall made of concrete slabs that reached twelve-feet above the ground. In the East, this wall was the second wall. The first wall on the Eastern side was the three-mile-wide wall that was built of invisible threat.

On the Eastern side, the third wall was a signal fence running 736 miles long and six and a half feet high. This wall was a fence made of barbed wire lined with low-voltage electrified strands. If the third wall were touched, a silent alarm would whisper to guards nearby.

The fourth wall was a "protective strip" 1,600 to 3,300 feet wide that adjoined the border itself. It was guarded, eventually, by almost 700 watchtowers and 12,000 border guards. The fourth wall was made of concrete and steel and wood and guns and eyes.

There was a wall of dogs and a wall of road and a blinding wall of light. There was a wall that was a carpet of steel spikes that could impale a potential crosser, and a wall that was a trench. There was a wall of steel anti-vehicle obstacles known as Czech hedgehogs that looked like miniature ziggurats. During the Second World War the Germans called these strange constructions 'dragon's teeth'. The Wall was forged of war ruins and storefronts and whatever the government could find. Torn-up gravestones from the Hedwig Cemetery paved the road inside the "death strip."

There was a twenty-to-fifty-foot-wide wall of sand illuminated by floodlights. Guards kept the sand cleanly raked to show off potential footprints. The pattern on the sand was not unlike that in a Zen rock garden. Stripped bare of growing things that are temporary and fragile, rock gardens are places to meditate on the true substance of the reality that lies beyond appearances. Zen monks will sometimes rake lines in the sand to mimic the undulating waves of streams. We are forever manipulating our environment, say the gardens, to reflect our ephemeral desires. But look closely at the lines and you will see that the sand is still just sand.

***

From the sky, the Wall once again entered the no-man's land between psychology and substance. "Where does the state end," asked Peter Schneider in his novel *The Wall Jumper*, "and a self begin?"

From a homemade hot air balloon in the dead of night, for instance, you would only make out a few lights. The course of the Wall looked hazy—wrote former East German Günter Wetzel of his family's famous border escape—and got hazier as the balloon spun around. Soon, you would lose your bearings entirely. But no matter where you floated in the dark, the presence of the Wall would remain. Later, you would only know for certain you had reached the West when you saw an unfamiliar piece of farm machinery. The last thing you would notice before you crashed to the ground were the treetops swaying in the wind.

From the sky, wrote Peter Schneider, you couldn't tell East from West. "Seen from the air, the city appears perfectly homogenous. Nothing suggests to the stranger that he is nearing a region where two political continents divide." From an airplane, he wrote,

> ...the wall in its fantastic zigzag course seems to be the figment of some anarchic imagination. Lit up in the afternoon by the setting sun and lavishly illuminated by floodlights after dark, the wall seems more a civic monument than a border.
>
> On a clear day the traveler can watch the plane's shadow skimming back and forth across the city. He can track the plane closing in on its shadow until it touches down right on top of it. Only when he disembarks does he notice that in this city, the recovered shadow signifies a loss. After the fact, he realizes that only the plane's shadow was free to move between the two parts of the city....

***

From America the Wall was television, and had always been that way. On the November 9, 1989 episode, the Wall was falling down. German people were running in and out of the Wall, and jumping around it, and singing, and crying. East and West Berliners were pulling each other on top of the Wall—it was important to be on top of the

Wall. A man in a suit was pounding the Wall with a small hammer, determined to take it down. Another man came and lifted him up so that the destruction could start at the top. Other footage showed the East Berlin police carrying away slumping East Berliners on stretchers and in their arms. It was not clear, said an American news reporter, if these people were drunk or being arrested. "When might the Wall come down?" another reporter asked the Deputy Mayor of West Berlin. She told him that the fall of the Wall would begin with a psychological dismantling.

As the television played in the background of America someone said, "I never thought I'd see the end of Communism." Soon after, the Wall was dust.

***

From Potsdamer Platz, you can now follow traces of the Wall via the "Berlin Wall Orientation System." Without the informational markers it is hard to get one's bearings. Most of the Wall is memory and a visitor or a child might not realize it was ever there at all. In some places, chunks of the Wall have been left standing; in others, the Wall has become maps or listening stations or photographs of its former self. There are periodic exhibitions on the history of the Wall on the Wall, or documentation of the Nazi era. A surviving watchtower near Stresemannstraße is now a "panorama observation tower." From it, you pretend to be a guard and keep watch on the "enemy" West. On the East Side, the Wall has become an open-air painting gallery. A ¾-mile stretch of this wall has recently been replaced by luxury condominiums.

Underground, the foundations of buildings lost under

the Wall are still being uncovered. In 2010, archaeologists revealed the remains of Bernauer Straße 10a. Only fifty-three years old and twenty-five years gone, the Wall is an archaeological ruin.

In some places the Wall has simply become a line. A double row of bricks laid into the street marks the former border. As a visitor, it can be confusing to come upon these bricks; you do not know whether to step on them or over them. You find yourself looking down the road to see how far you would have to walk to go around them completely.

***

A wall casts a shadow between ground and sun. It is, therefore, like a gnomon, the wedge that makes the shadow on a sundial. As the shadow is not possible without the gnomon, the gnomon is also the shadow itself. In geometry, a gnomon is the part of a parallelogram that remains after a similar parallelogram has been removed from one of its corners. A gnomon is—like the Wall, like a memory – both presence and absence. This doesn't mean that shadow is the same as substance. Nor that shadow is unreal. Negative and positive, shadow and substance always work together. "How can I be substantial if I do not cast a shadow?" asked the psychologist Carl Jung. "I must have a dark side also if I am to be whole." The word 'gnomon' is derived from the Greek and literally means 'one who knows'. A gnomon is an indicator, a pointer, directed at both darkness and sun.

The shadow, wrote Jung, is that which each man despises in himself—the dark side. But it is also the darkness that lingers in the consciousness of a particular society. We often try to eliminate the shadows by ignoring the shadow-makers or trying to destroy them. But the shadows only disappear when shrouded in more darkness, and then, they are only hiding.

"It will take us longer to tear down the Wall in our heads than any wrecking company will need for the Wall we can see," Peter Schneider wrote.

"But the city outside, with its fire walls, garden walls, border walls—those walls will still be standing when no one is left to move beyond them."

Stefany Anne Golberg

Martha, Smithsonian (archive photo)

Martha

In the last years of her life, Martha began to lose her feathers. Sol Stephan, General Manager of the Cincinnati Zoo, where Martha spent most of her years, began collecting the feathers in a cigar box without much idea of what he would do with them. Martha lived a sedentary life at the zoo. Her cage was 18 feet by 20 feet—she had never known what it was to fly free. When Martha's last friend George (who was also named for a Washington) died in 1910, Martha became a celebrity. She watched the people passing by, alone in her enclosure, and they watched her. Martha ate her cooked liver and eggs, and her cracked corn, and sat. On the outside of her cage, Stephan placed a sign announcing Martha as the Last of the Passenger Pigeons. Visitors couldn't believe that Martha really was the last. They would throw sand inside the cage to make her walk around.

Martha died on a September afternoon in 1914. Her elderly body was sent to the Cincinnati Ice Company and frozen in a 300-pound block of ice. They put the frozen Martha on a train to the Smithsonian, where she could be mounted and stuffed. Martha was displayed at the Smithsonian between the 1920s and 1950s. For a while, she sat next to an unnamed male passenger pigeon that had been shot in 1873. Later, she was displayed alone. In her current arrangement, Martha's feathers look nice. Her head is turned in the gentle, curious way of pigeons. She stands on a branch, as if wild. Martha never stood this way in life, but in death she has taken on a new role: She is Martha the Last Passenger Pigeon. The specimen made from Martha's remains is among the Smithsonian's most treasured possessions.

***

The fall migrations of the Wild Pigeons, wrote the naturalist Charles Dury in 1910, were an impressive sight. In Cincinnati, he wrote, the birds liked to come out in the afternoon and evening, and generally when the day was cloudy. They flew in long columns or strings, side by side, very high in the sky. Sometimes the flocks would come together, he wrote, and would stretch from horizon to horizon. In seasons when the beechnuts were abundant, the passenger pigeons would come to the ground. They would eat the nuts until the nuts were gone, while some birds kept watch up above. Here, they were much easier to shoot, wrote Dury, though one could never slaughter so many as the professional pigeon trappers. For several years in succession, wrote Dury, a great flock came to the Blatchley woods, where I bagged as many as I could carry. Their method of eating the beechnuts was very interesting and peculiar, wrote Dury. The birds seemed to swallow them whole.

I have seen the birds sell as low as 25 cents per dozen on the Cincinnati market, wrote Dury in his *Reminiscence*, but

50 cents to $1.00 per dozen was the usual price. When the Cincinnati Zoo opened in 1875, they had a fine bunch of passenger pigeons—about 22 birds. Now, in 1910, wrote Dury, there are but two veritable patriarchs. The zoo tried to breed more pigeons, but they were not successful.

"One foggy day in October 1884, at 5am," wrote Dury, "I looked out of my bedroom window, and as I looked six wild pigeons flew down and perched on the dead branches of a tall poplar tree that stood about one hundred feet away. As I gazed at them in delight, feeling as though old friends had come back, they quickly darted away and disappeared in the fog, the last I ever saw of any of these birds in this vicinity."

***

At some point in your life, a bird will come to you. Looking at this bird will help you to see all the other birds. It was a brown bird that came to nest on my fire escape in Brooklyn, maybe nine years ago. The bird built a nest on my window ledge and put two white eggs inside. I did not see this nest construction; the nest just appeared. Later that day, the bird came to be with the nest. She didn't do anything to the nest, just stood alongside it, and when she looked at me looking at her, I really saw, for the first time in my life, a bird. And what I noticed too, when I looked at the brown bird (which I later understood to be a mourning dove—that is to say, a pigeon) was its silent way. It is their abundance and their silence that makes the pigeons invisible.

***

There is a difference between the rock pigeon and the passenger pigeon. The passenger pigeon was in America before we were; the rock pigeon was Europe's gift. The rock pigeon dwells in our cities and is mostly left alone. The passenger pigeon flocked everywhere, and was brought to the cities dead. The word 'passenger'—as in passenger pigeon —was once interchangeable with 'wild'. Rock pigeons are wild too, only wild like the streets. They drift around parks and thoroughfares, looking for scraps and bones.

'Passenger' was derived from the French word 'passager', which means to pass on by. The passenger pigeon was a nomad; the entirety of America was its home. We named them passenger pigeons because of the way the birds would leave and then suddenly come together in a great mass to breed. Every year, the pigeons turned up someplace new and by the billions. They say it was a spectacular sight. In autumn of 1813, along the banks of the Ohio River, the birdist John James Audubon sat down on a rock to study passenger pigeons. He took out a pencil and marked a dot for every flock that passed. In twenty-one minutes, Audubon realized the absurdity of his task. One hundred and sixty-three dots in twenty-one minutes—a "countless multitude" of pigeons. "I traveled on, and still met more the farther I proceeded," he wrote. "The air was literally filled with Pigeons." The afternoon sun was blotted from the sky; the bird dung fell like snow. By sunset Audubon had traveled fifty-five miles and the clouds of pigeons kept passing. They continued to pass without stopping for three more days.

***

A passenger pigeon could be used for just about any commodity; every part was useful. Its feathers made decent bedding; its blood was good for the eyes. Its dung could cure a headache and, for dysentery, a dose of powdered pigeon stomach. The plentiful meat of a pigeon was served to the slave, and after slavery, the poor, and to pigs.

The gregarious passenger pigeon would only court in flocks, in the company of fellow birds. It's the reason that captives refused to breed—they disliked private love. Perhaps if the birds had been more discreet they would have been harder to shoot. Some say the passenger pigeon was a rare sight when the European arrived, and grew in number with the devastation of Native Americans. The birds were no longer eaten by the Natives and no longer had to compete with them for food.

***

In ancient times, you could decipher the will of the gods by studying the ways of the birds. Every aspect of a bird guided people to act in accordance with the divine. The quality of sound a bird made—the pitch of its voice or the direction it was coming from—the way the birds were eating that day, the tilt of their heads from this way to that, the subtle shifts of feathers and peeps; all of these were signs. Each species of bird had something different to say—owls and ravens were particularly prophetic, as were eagles and woodpeckers and vultures. The Roman armies carried sacred chickens in the field, to watch the chickens eat. When the chickens ate so much the food fell out of their faces, the soldiers knew fortune was smiling.

The bird priest, the augur, paid close attention to the sky, to watch how the birds were flying. Were they gathered or alone? Did they fly up or across? Were the birds at rest and if so, where? Which parts of the sky were the birds in today? How did the birds seem to feel?

On the morning of New Years' Day in 2011, around 4,000 blackbirds fell from the sky. Dead birds lay twisted in the streets of Beebe, Arkansas, in church parking lots and backyards. Later, after they had collected the fallen birds, autopsies showed the cause of death as blunt force trauma. Something in the night had terrified the birds; in the dark, they left the trees. They flew blindly into cars and buildings and telephone poles and each other. Authorities blamed the mass death on fireworks at first, though no one knew for sure. Maybe a lightening storm spooked the birds, some said, or a colossal torrent of hail. The residents of Beebe picked up the birds and moved forward. Only, the following New Year's, the birds fell again, and again by the thousands. The weather that New Year's evening had been calm in Beebe, and the police placed a ban on fireworks. And no one could explain why, a few days after the initial blackbird deaths in Beebe, hundreds of birds had also dropped dead on a highway in Baton Rouge. Some Americans conjectured about the end of days. Some about poisoned air. Some said that birds get together and die en masse all the time.

In ancient times, the augur never advised what action should be taken after reading the signs of the birds. Nor could an augur say what the outcome of any action would be. Augury was a form of divination, but the augur couldn't tell the future. The birds told the augur whether the decisions human beings had already made would please or anger the gods. It was then up to people to choose whether they wanted to trust or ignore the birds.

"Not a whit, we defy augury," Hamlet tells Horatio, after Horatio warns Hamlet he will lose his duel with Laertes. "There's a special providence in the fall of a sparrow. If it be now, 'tis not to come; if it be not to come, it will be now; if it be not now, yet it will come: the readiness is all: since no man has aught of what he leaves, what is't to leave betimes?" We can't escape fate, says Hamlet. When the sparrow falls, why not accept the message, and therefore accept providence, whatever it be? The readiness is all.

On the morning before the great sea-battle of Drepanum between Carthage and the Roman Republic in 249 BC, the chickens refused to eat. The horrified Roman crew looked to their general, who scrambled for a different interpretation. "Then let them drink," said Publius Claudius Pulcher, and threw the chickens overboard. The Romans went into battle in spite of the birds and, naturally, were defeated.

***

Placed between Gorilla World, Cat House, and World of the Insect at the Cincinnati Zoo is an aviary pagoda. That's where Martha spent her final days. There are three stuffed passenger pigeons on display in the pagoda, alongside Incas, the last captive Carolina Parakeet. Incas died at the museum in 1918, inside Martha's cage. On the path to the pagoda, a bronze memorial statue of Martha stands frozen on a rock. Her head is cocked and she's walking toward something. Or, she could be walking away.

Boredom

We wish we could make it go away, the horrible, oppressive boredom. But the more we fight boredom the more powerful it becomes. Every activity is a diversion, every pleasure a ruse. All the fun things we do in opposition to boredom become fantastically, inevitably boring. Sometimes we try to locate those things that bore us and yawn them out of our lives. That woman, that radio program, that political agenda—they are so boring! We pretend we can cure the boredom, knowing all the while that Kierkegaard was right. There is a fundamental tedium lurking in every moment. Anything, anyone, at any time, can become suddenly and unexpectedly boring.

"We've been bored since the very beginning," wrote Kierkegaard.

> The gods were bored; therefore they created human beings. Adam was bored because he was alone; therefore Eve was created.... then Adam and Eve were bored together; then Adam and Eve and Cain and Abel were bored *en famille*. After that the population of the world increased, and the nations were bored *en masse*. To amuse themselves they hit upon the no-

> tion of building a tower so high that it would reach the sky. This notion is just as boring as the tower was high, and is a terrible demonstration of how boredom gained the upper hand. Then they were dispersed around the world, just as people now travel abroad, but they continued to be bored.

The realization that boredom was insatiable led Kierkegaard to an oft-quoted truth: Boredom is the root of all evil. Nero burned Rome to ashes at the height of his powers simply because he was bored. But what delayed the fall of Rome? asked Kierkegaard in *Rotation of Crops*. Bread and circus, games, amusements. Traveling, battles, exploration, romance—the usual panaceas for boredom. Or, at the other end of the spectrum, we become hardworking and diligent, thinking we can outsmart the boredom by denying pleasure altogether. But the impulse is still the same. Always the diversion comes with more questions than answers: What now? What else? What more? Diversion, diversion, diversion. It's the only way we know to alleviate the pain. For boredom is painful. That's what Kierkegaard really meant when he said that boredom is the root of all evil. The bored person looks harmless enough. Peaceful even sometimes. But inside the bored person lurks a terror. In the throes of boredom, we are confronted with the darkest part of existence.

The philosopher Schopenhauer had his own take on boredom. He described human existence as unceasing striving through an endless series of transient moments. We want to stop and reflect, to make the transience more substantial—but we don't know how to stop. We only find pleasure when we are striving after something. Life, wrote Schopenhauer, is "a man running down a mountain who would fall over if he tried to stop and can stay on his feet only by running on." We think the whole point of our lives is striving. When we accomplish our goals, we feel good. But the accomplishment is as temporary as the striving; the instant we have what we wanted, it is boring. We are then faced with another terrible truth: striving is meaningless. And there is more. If life is striving, then life is meaningless—the boredom itself is the proof. If life possessed any real value, boredom would not exist. Just existing would satisfy us.

"Boredom rests upon the nothingness that winds its way through existence," wrote Kierkegaard, "its dizziness is infinite, like that which comes from looking down into a bottomless abyss." Kierkegaard had a name for a life defined by enjoyment and diversion—he called it the aesthetic life. If you are not a reflective person, you might get away with comfortably living out your days in the endless cycle of boredom and distraction. But if you have a tendency toward self-reflection, and you think that reflection will save you from boredom, you are in trouble. For all you will see is an empty abyss, the dark heart of nothingness. For you, the aesthetic life will only lead to despair.

***

In the last years of his life, Giacomo Chevalier De Seingalt Casanova was a librarian. The famed libertine had no money, no friends. His reputation was destroyed; his body was exhausted from decades of wine and venereal disease. Casanova was in a desperate state when he met Count Waldstein in Paris. The Count found Casanova amusing, and decided to make Casanova his personal librarian at the

Castle Dux, where Casanova spent the last fourteen years of his life. Casanova despised the other members of the Dux household—the way they prepared the coffee was wrong. They couldn't make decent macaroni to save their lives. He was certain the kitchen served his soup boiling hot just to annoy him. Once at the castle, the Count mostly ignored Casanova—Casanova, a man who had spoken with all the crowned heads of Europe. Casanova hated being poor, hated being dependent, hated being lonely. But he was old and the ancien regime was dead. In despair, and bored beyond all hope, Casanova considered suicide. But he didn't have the constitution for it. Casanova resigned himself to writing his memoirs instead.

Casanova was born into the most extraordinary milieu—the Republic of Venice in the 18th century, pleasure capital of Europe. At nine years old, his parents discarded him; at eleven he was fondled and enlightened by the pretty, light-hearted Bettina. He entered the university at seventeen, studied law, moral philosophy, chemistry, mathematics. At seventeen Casanova discovered fashion, became a man-about-town and a dandy. He discovered gambling, had his first sexual experience, was admitted as an abbé by the church, lost all his money, had his first prison experience, was dismissed by the church, and started looking for a new profession all before the age of twenty. Casanova spent the rest of his life searching. The searching took the form of intrigues and prison breaks, seduction and wealth, prostitution and Rosicrucianism, blasphemies, music, scandal, fame.

Casanova wanted no one's tears—his merits and faults were all his own. "Whatever I have done in the course of my life," wrote Casanova in his memoirs, "whether it be good or evil, has been done freely." Every debt, every cuckold, every reputation Casanova ruined including his own, even his boredom were products of his fundamental freedom. How pleasant it is, Casanova wrote to his imaginary audience, to converse with myself about myself, and to make myself laugh. If you are kind you will laugh with me, he wrote. In any case, Casanova told his future readers, I think you will find me more virtuous than not.

The Preface to Casanova's memoirs is usually referred to as the unremorseful, confessional part of *The Story of My Life*, if it is read at all. The Preface contains Casanova's metaphysics: Well-considered but unfettered diversion was the path to enlightenment. Man is born free in order to wage war against boredom. Despite his failed church career, Casanova was a religious man, a Christian to the end. The war against boredom was thus a holy crusade for Casanova. "Man is free," wrote Casanova, "but his freedom ceases when he has no faith in it." To have faith in freedom is to grasp every bit of it, to freely pursue every last woman and tasty morsel on the planet. God gave free will to man and also pleasure—to deny either was to deny God. "Insane are those who fancy that the Almighty can enjoy the sufferings....which they offer to Him as a sacrifice.... All he has given unto us has been intended for our happiness." To love God was to live for happiness, for pleasure and for freedom. Casanova, by his own account, was especially born for good living. "The chief business of my life," he wrote, "has been to indulge my senses." Casanova loved the smell of strong cheese and strong women; he was passionate and curious and courageous. To be anything less would be boring.

"Oh, cruel ennui!" Casanova lamented at the end. "It

must be by mistake that those who have invented the torments of hell have forgotten to ascribe thee the first place among them." When Casanova was no longer able to indulge his senses, he fell into the agony of boredom. Writing his memoirs was Casanova's very last pleasure and yet writing them was so boring! Casanova resented ending his days as a writer, embalming a lifetime of amusement for the grave of posterity. But he did it for the rest of us, to teach us how to conquer boredom in God's name. Casanova saw his life as the fulfillment of a philosophy: "My errors will point to thinking men the various roads, and will teach them the great art of treading on the brink of the precipice without falling into it."

***

The whole secret to defeating boredom, Kierkegaard wrote, is arbitrariness. People usually think it is easy to be arbitrary, but it is actually a studied affair.

> One does not enjoy the immediate object but something else that one arbitrarily introduces. One sees the middle of a play; one reads the third section of a book. One thereby has enjoyment quite different from what the author so kindly intended. One enjoys something totally accidental; one considers the whole of existence from this standpoint; one lets its reality run aground on this.

With arbitrariness you transform the accidental into the absolute. The only way to truly transcend the dreaded abyss of boredom is therefore by leaping, irrationally, into the arms of the infinite—namely, the arms of God. By giving ourselves over to the accidental, the mysterious, we are less prone to control our experience, to trick ourselves into believing that we can think our way out of boredom. When we throw ourselves to God, Kierkegaard said, we give ourselves over to the unknown, because God is totally incomprehensible. Standing before the abyss with God, we can finally see our true selves.

Ultimately, Kierkegaard and Casanova agreed: Boredom is the problem. Boredom is a spiritual malady and is rooted in an emptiness of the soul. But do we transcend boredom by living with and for diversion like Casanova or by moving beyond it like Kierkegaard? There seems to be a hair's breadth of difference separating the two remedies. Kierkegaard leaped away from the aesthetic path and Casanova leaped fully into it.

Both men were living testaments to their respective philosophies. Both gave up any notion of marriage or family life or community, believing that domestic trifles would hinder the search for a truly meaningful life. Casanova traveled everywhere, Kierkegaard traveled nowhere, and both ended their days essentially as exiles, in isolation, ridiculed and scorned by the public. Kierkegaard—who sacrificed love for truth—died young at 42, miserable. Casanova – who sacrificed everything for pleasure—died old at 73, bored. They say the Venetian playboy's last words were, "I have lived as a philosopher and I die as a Christian."

Giacomo Casanova's narrative of adventure and exploit was never finished—he stopped abruptly at Volume Twelve. It is, perhaps, better that way. Anyone who has ever tried to get through all twelve volumes of Giacomo Casanova's life story will agree. After the first seven volumes or so, the story gets a little boring.

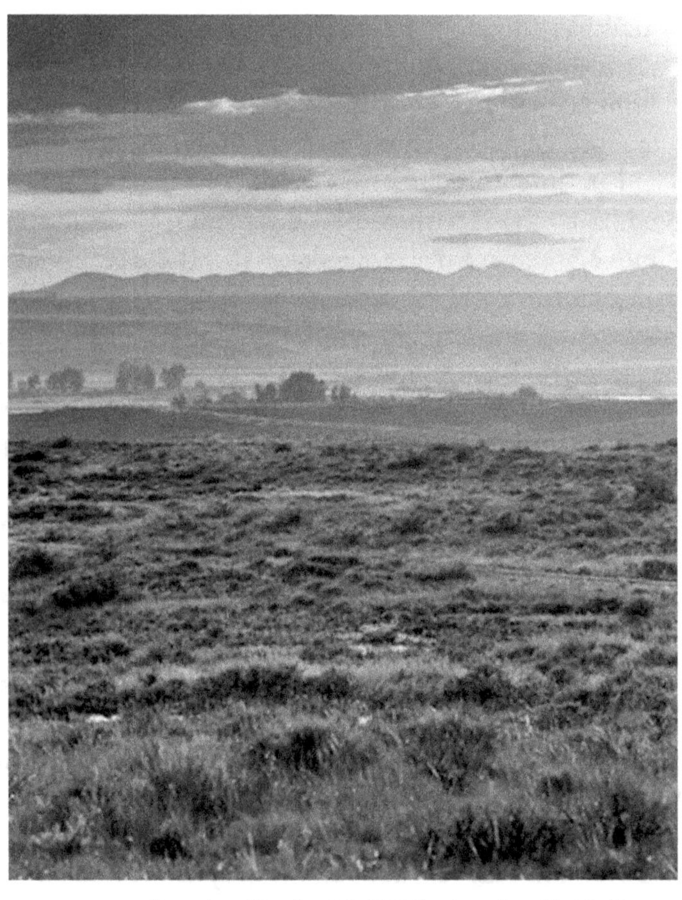

Posted on October 19, 2012 by American Prairie Reserve

The Prairie

Underneath the great long land of the Prairie the grass grows down. It grows into the darkness. It tangles into itself, roots into itself, is a labyrinth of roots that holds the soil firmly overhead with its trillions of tentacles and won't easily be convinced to let go. The Prairie doesn't beg for water like other landscapes do. She doesn't pray for a storm blown in from elsewhere to rain life down upon her. The Prairie knows how to live thirsty. She can persist if necessary through years of drought, bolstering herself on her own provisions. The Prairie knows how to wait. And when the Prairie at last gets bored of thirst, she sends out her roots in search of a drink, cabling them out far and wide. In the wintertime the Prairie likes to play dead, she looks dead to onlookers. If a fire comes and overtakes the trees and thistle, the Prairie seems doomed. But this is mostly a ruse. For every ten-foot strand of tall grass you can see, there are ten more feet you can't. So long as her maze of matter thrives below the ground, you know that she is still breathing. If you dig up her grasses, and dig up her roots, and you plant something daintier in their place, the Prairie loses more than her scouts. She loses her very reason for being, and will scowl and hold her breath until the rains come, if they come, as the daintier plants shrivel and fade.

When roots die inside the Prairie, the decomposers slowly eat them, feeding the soil in kind. The Prairie is land that feeds on itself, *causa sui*, needing no one. The Prairies came to life in the shadows of mountains, the Rocky Mountains to be exact. As the Rockies grew higher, they cast more darkness over the trees that stood below them. The trees died, along with the creatures that love trees. In their place, a graveyard of grass. The open sky brought wind and the sun brought fire and the stiff grasses flourished under the assault. The Prairie is a desert that looks like a meadow. It is a French word, prairie, French for 'meadow', though as Bishop William Alfred Quayle was quick to point out, the Prairie is no French meadow. A meadow in France is a playground for girls picking purple wildflowers. It is a sheep's paradise, a cow's castle, a field where soldiers write poems about themselves before they crushingly, heroically, fall. The grasses of the Prairie have names like porcupine, rough fescue, sand reed, and needle-and-thread. The grasses of France need people to tend them. The prairie grasses live best without us.

The late Pleistocene brought the bison, the last great emperors of the Prairie, with their thick Viking beards and wild hair. They were the most tremendous of the continent's mammals, larger than grizzlies—the mountains of the Plains. Their foreheads alone were monuments. The bison enveloped the whole of the Prairie, and the Prairie once sounded like rolling thunder under the hulking footfall of millions of bison. Prehistory lingered in the bodies of the bison, they were ancient until their kingdom's demise. The teeth of the bison never evolved into blades, as true kings need no weapons. They turned the Prairie soil with their feet, and munched on wild lilies and shrubs.

The settlers eliminated the bison from the Prairie to make way for their farms, it's been written, though some say it was to punish the Natives. Actually, what scared settlers most was that their domesticated cows would mix blood with the hairy beasts of the Plain, and recapture the ancestry they lost long before in the plaintive meadows of Europe.

The bison had people to keep them company—the Cree, the Dakota, the Blackfoot, the Lakota. The early people were nomads, travelers. They rolled through the Prairie and lived for each day, building no statues, planting no fruit. The First Nations built fires in the grass, to shift the Prairie's organization and make it more they way they liked it. The fires helped the Natives manage their crops and lure the animals. But sometimes the fires slipped out of their hands and flooded the Prairie in flame. Settlements were burned and people were burned and the burned parts of the Prairie were useless. The animals they sought were driven away, and signal fires signaled wildly.

In some parts, the Prairie gets tired and stops, and breaks into a line of cliffs. Bones have been found at the bottoms of cliffs, thirty feet thick and going for miles. The cliffs were the slaughterhouses of the hunters of the Plains. One hunter who had a gift for crying would gather near a bison herd. He would cry out like a lost calf and bring the bison to attention. The bison would follow the sound of the calf, getting closer toward the cliff's edge. At the right moment, the rest of the hunters would scream and circle around the bison. The bison would be pushed further and further toward the cliff, until it was too late. The weight of the stampede behind forced the first bison over the precipice—the rest lost balance and followed. At the bottom, the bison lay helpless in a pile with crushed bodies and legs. The tribesmen below, who had watched the creatures drop, bludgeoned them one by one. The Blackfoot had a name for these places. They called them deep blood kettle.

The tribes of the Plains performed a Sun Dance ceremony that lasted for many days. They made an altar of a buffalo skull and presented the skull with gifts. The Dakota were sure that the bones of the bison would rise again with new flesh for the tribe. They put great stock in the bones of animals and people; they thought that the soul was inside the bones. It was an honor to be reduced to bones. When a living thing was reduced to nothing but bones it entered back into the primordial cycle of life. Bones are the continuity between life and death. When the ceremony was done, the tribe moved on, and the bones left to Nature's will.

The first Europeans to look upon the Prairies wrote that the sight made them sick. These were fur traders, adventurers, hard men on the run, professional butchers not generally prone to weak stomachs. In the emptiness of the desert, one's thought can turn to the divine. The Prairie, however, is just Nature, Nature at her most elemental. The wind pushed the white men all around, slapped them around and kicked the backs of their knees so that they could hardly stand, so that they could hardly breathe. The Prairie wind made them feel they were on a sinking ship, and they were lonely. So very lonely.

The Europeans hunted through the tall dry grass, looking for animals and Natives. All throughout the landscape they came across stones that had been stacked and placed in rings. They thought that the rings were the foundations of teepees, put there by the Cree. Later, they found skeletons underneath the stones. The circles were not meant for the living.

The last pioneers came to the Prairie to make her their Garden of Eden. They plowed the grass that was of no value to them and planted crops in their place. They imported animals and planted flowers and fruit, they built temples and played gay songs. They turned the yellow Prairie grass into a land of gold. "How beautiful are the fields afterwards when they become green," a pioneer wrote in a letter. "This draws you and draws you and makes you willing to root our forests, turn over fields, even drink the sweat that pours from your forehead, and yet be satisfied." The Prairie was a glorious garden for a decade or so. A paradise to behold.

In the 1930s, everything was turned back to wind and sand, and the Prairie brought her ancient fragments to the surface. They were mostly bits of pottery, some from 10,000 years back, and there were also tools and bones. The bones were not prehistoric, as people thought they might be. They were the bones of the white men, the traders and explorers, men who were escaping and men who wandered, never dreaming their bodies would get left behind, buried on the Plains right where they died, in a shallow grave of dust. In the 1930s, the immigrants found the bones of the refugees and wondered how their own bones would be found. Then they gathered the shards and tried to sell them for whatever they could get. With not much to do for fun and no money to be made, the collecting of remains became a popular Prairie pastime. Time moved neither backward nor forward during the dry days of Depression.

They plowed more, looking to dig up more secrets. But

nothing was there. The grasses of the Prairie have no power of resurrection, said the Bishop William Alfred Quayle. They have no seeds, no flowers, and they can't be planted again. The Prairie grasses have only roots and once plowed, they are destroyed.

In Hebrew scripture it is written that humans will one day return to Eden, the place where humans began. When they do, the story of humans will come full circle and history, at last, will end. The Hebrews got the word Eden from an Akkadian word that comes from a Sumerian word meaning 'plains'. If only the last pioneers had realized before they started that Eden is only a prairie.

THE DEVIL'S DICTIONARY

An early edition of *The Devil's Dictionary,* Drawings by J. C. Suares

Devil's Dictionary

> CYNIC, n. A blackguard whose faulty vision sees things as they are, not as they ought to be. Hence the custom among the Scythians of plucking out a cynic's eyes to improve his vision.

In 1906, a book written by the infamous curmudgeon Ambrose Bierce was published as *The Cynic's Word Book.* It was Bierce's preference that the book—a collection of satirical definitions which he had written for various newspapers "in a desultory way at long intervals" from 1881 to 1906—be called *The Devil's Dictionary*, but the anti-religious implications of the title made publishers nervous.

In 1906, American bookshelves were flooded with "a score of 'cynic' books—*The Cynic's This, The Cynic's That, The Cynic's t'Other,* to name a few. As far as those other "cynic" books were concerned, Bierce added, "most" were "merely stupid, though some of them added the distinction of silliness. Among them, they brought the word 'cynic' into disfavor so deep that any book bearing it was discredited in advance of publication." As Bierce wrote his definitions for various newspapers columns over the years, they had appeared under a variety of names: *The Cynic's Diction-*

ary, The Demon's Dictionary, The Cynic's Word Book. But no title was ever as satisfying as the one he finally demanded.

On the surface, it's unclear why cynicism was such a popular attitude in those years padding the front and back ends of the turn of the century. It was decades past the Civil War and years before the First World War. America had started to grow comfortable in her role as a country that was powerful but not so powerful as to shoulder the burden of being a real global force. Progress was fast becoming the new religion, giving Americans a sense of excitement about their place in the universe. Americans put on wonderful exhibitions about their own wonderful inventions—light bulbs, remote control technology, the telephone, the Ferris wheel—while not yet feeling the full invasion of technology and amusement that would define the 20th century.

Yet with all this optimism came a sense of unease. It had been a while since Americans, as a whole, had felt anything to be at stake. Americans were brought together socially by the Civil War and light bulbs, but they were also becoming unmoored from the traditions that once gave them a sense of community. Cynicism was a way to discuss the growing emptiness of American life and the coming disorientation of modernity with an easy hilarity—cynicism for cynicism's sake.

It was to Bierce's annoyance that he found himself persistently and flagrantly plagiarized by all those lesser writers out there trying to make their livings as cynics. No doubt, Bierce's writings were smarter and funnier than the stupid, distinctively silly cynic books of his time. He was a satirist of the first order. But Bierce was angered by these people because he saw himself as no mere humorist, no dandy wit seeking cheap titters from parlor rooms. Rather, Bierce saw himself as a voice of authority and a harbinger of truth. No one was safe from his verbal blitz. It's amazing that any newspaper ever employed Ambrose Bierce, who readily showered his bile on anyone and anything in society he deemed hypocritical—which was just about everyone and everything. *The Devil's Dictionary* was an attack on politics, philosophy, the aristocracy. For example, a POLITICIAN was:

> An eel in the fundamental mud upon which the superstructure of organized society is reared. When he wriggles he mistakes the agitation of his tail for the trembling of the edifice. As compared with the statesman, he suffers the disadvantage of being alive.

While a LORD was "In American society, an English tourist above the state of a costermonger.... sometimes used, also, as a title of the Supreme Being."

Bierce defined a MONAD as a little gentleman destined to evolve into "a German philosopher of the first class," not to be confused with a MICROBE, "an entirely distinct species." LOVE was "A temporary insanity curable by marriage or by removal of the patient from the influences under which he incurred the disorder," while HATRED was a "sentiment appropriate to the occasion of another's superiority." Even the medium of *The Devil's Dictionary* itself was an excuse for a quip:

> DICTIONARY, n. A malevolent literary device for cramping the growth of a language and making it hard and inelastic.

Though Bierce was quick to add: "This dictionary, however, is a most useful work."

Just as devastating were his, shall we call them, metaphysical critiques. Bierce had no patience for those who acted badly in the name of faith. Bierce claimed to have no religious convictions himself; he only cared "a good deal for truth, reason, and fair play." (You can tell a lot about a man's metaphysics when he classifies GOOD as an adjective instead of a noun.) Bierce defined WORSHIP as "Homo Creator's testimony to the sound construction and fine finish of Deus Creatus. A popular form of abjection, having an element of pride." FAITH was "Belief without evidence in what is told by one who speaks without knowledge, of things without parallel." His definition of WRATH implicated everyone from priests to kings to worshipers:

> WRATH, n. Anger of a superior quality and degree, appropriate to exalted characters and momentous occasions; as, "the wrath of God," "the day of wrath," etc. Amongst the ancients the wrath of kings was deemed sacred, for it could usually command the agency of some god for its fit manifestation, as could also that of a priest.... God is now Love, and a director of the census performs his work without apprehension of disaster.

Cynicism, for Bierce, was not just an attitude; it was his life force. It's ironic then that *The Devil's Dictionary* is seen today primarily as a delightful little book of irreverent (if anachronistic) witticisms. This is entirely Bierce's fault. In life and in art, Bierce made it his prerogative to present himself as a misanthropic know-it-all. Much of the real sensitivity and even anguish that produced *The Devil's Dic-*

tionary is obscured by an intentional ironic distance.

By the time *The Devil's Dictionary* was published, Bierce was 69. He had made a career as a curmudgeon, a writer with a big personality who always kept distance between himself and his public. He was famous for his motto "nothing matters" and was known as "Bitter Bierce." Even his popular short stories, based on his experiences of the Civil War (see the classic "An Occurrence at Owl Creek Bridge") were never autobiographical, never meant to bring readers closer to the man. He publicly attacked friends, employers and, of course, other writers. (Bierce had a literary run-in with Oscar Wilde once after the latter declared satire to be "as sterile as it is shameful, and as impotent as it is insolent." Bierce responded in print, calling Wilde "a gawky gowk," a "dunghill he-hen," and the "littlest and looniest of a brotherhood of simpletons" who had "the divine effrontery to link his name with those of Swindburne, Rosetti and Morris.") How could someone who addressed his book to "those…enlightened souls who prefer dry wines to sweet, sense to sentiment, wit to humor and clean English to slang" be taken all that seriously? Today, *The Devil's Dictionary* comes off as smart but smug. Who was Ambrose Bierce to pronounce such judgments on humanity?

> HISTORY, n. An account mostly false, of events mostly unimportant, which are brought about by rulers mostly knaves, and soldiers mostly fools.

Despite his attempts to obscure it, Bierce's autobiography is key to understanding *The Devil's Dictionary*. Ambrose Bierce was born in what his biographer Roy Morris calls the "ramshackle religious community of Horse Creek Cave,

Ohio." The site of Bierce's childhood, writes Morris, was "a hotbed of revivalist frenzy, full of spirit-rappers, tongue-talkers, stump-shouters, and psalm-singers." His parents ("unwashed savages," Bierce called them) were very poor and very pious. They ran a large household of 13 children, none of whom Bierce felt close to. In this milieu, the sensitive and serious Bierce was lost, and his sadness translated quickly to bitterness. Even as a child, the passion Bierce had for the Truth outweighed his sympathy for human weakness. As a child, Bierce once asked his mother to verify the existence of Santa Claus. Of course there is a Santa Claus, his mother assured him. But Bierce was soon to discover, as all children will, the horrible reality. It was this, Bierce said years later, that cemented the deep and irreparable betrayal of his mother: "I proceeded forthwith to detest my deceiver with all my little might and main."

Yet inside the Bierce home was a secret treasure—his father's library, said to be the largest in the county. It was here that the Bierce family's 10th child found refuge. ("A man of considerable scholarship," Bierce said of his father. "All that I have," he said, "I owe to his books.") In this complicated household, Bierce experienced profoundly the tensions between religion and reason, truth and fiction, knowledge and faith. Lacking any sense of belonging, Bierce became rebellious, idealistic, and angry. He resented his upbringing; resented the angry hollers of the self-appointed men of God that designed sermons to terrify boys; resented living in small-minded, small-town America; resented the poverty and the convention.

Bierce began adulthood early. At the age of 15, he left the family farm to work as a "printer's devil" for an abolitionist newspaper, and throughout his teens supported himself through odd jobs he thought beneath him. But the event that would most define the young Bierce was the Civil War, which began when he was 19. Bierce immediately enlisted, "sufficiently zealous for Freedom" and with a youthful excitement for the romance of battle. What he saw instead was evil. Unlike many other writers of his day, who would write eloquently of the war at arm's length, Bierce was a real soldier and lived the soldier's horror. Any last shreds of idealism he may have had about the goodness of humanity were buried at Philippi and Shiloh. Later, in between his more satirical newspaper columns, Bierce continued again and again to put his demons into words:

> Dead horses were everywhere; a few disabled caissons, or limbers, reclining on one elbow, as it were; ammunition wagons standing disconsolate behind four or six sprawling mules. Men? There were men enough; all dead apparently, except one, who lay near where I had halted my platoon to await the slower movement of the line—a Federal sergeant, variously hurt, who had been a fine giant in his time. He lay face upward, taking in his breath in convulsive, rattling snorts, and blowing it out in sputters of froth which crawled creamily down his cheeks, piling itself alongside his neck and ears. A bullet had clipped a groove in his skull, above the temple; from this the brain protruded in bosses, dropping off in flakes and strings. I had not previously known one could get on, even in this unsatisfactory fashion, with so little brain. One of my men whom I knew for a womanish fellow, asked if he should put his bayonet through him. Inexpressibly shocked by the cold-blooded proposal, I told him I thought not; it

> was unusual, and too many were looking.
> —*from* "What I Saw of Shiloh" *(1862)*

These stories, though, were never quite as popular as his satire.

Bierce himself was badly wounded in the war. He received honors for heroism (contrary to the character in the above story, for rescuing a wounded soldier in battle). But his injuries, physical and otherwise, would plague Bierce for the rest of his life. And though he just made it out of the war alive, one gets the feeling he wished he hadn't.

Demons haunted Bierce's personal life, too. He married and bore three children, yet felt oppressed by conventions of family life. Bierce would spend long cold stretches of time away from his wife Mollie, feeling her to be an unsuitable match. In 1888, Bierce found a stack of love letters addressed to Mollie from a stranger and accused her (falsely) of infidelity. He abandoned her after 17 years of marriage, cutting her off as abruptly as he had his mother years before. In letters, he referred to Mollie as "wife" and "Mrs. B." In 1904, Bierce filed for divorce; Mollie died alone the next year, before the proceedings could go through. He once told his daughter that Mollie was the only woman he ever loved. Bierce would also witness the death of both his sons. The eldest, Day, was shot in a gunfight over his fiancé, who had left him for another; the second son, Leigh, died of pneumonia related to alcoholism.

> MAN, n. An animal so lost in rapturous contemplation of what he thinks he is as to overlook what he indubitably ought to be. His chief occupation is extermination of other animals and his own species, which, however, multiplies with such insistent

> rapidity as to infest the whole habitable earth and Canada.

Bierce's definition of CYNIC as "a blackguard whose faulty vision sees things as they are, not as they ought to be" is easily dismissed as the rant of a self-important curmudgeon. But Bierce had seen America in the depths of hell, had seen love from the bottom of a pit. He had shaken hands with greedy governors and jaded journalists, saw how men and women could abuse each other in the name of freedom and justice and altruism. For all its humor, *The Devil's Dictionary* is a damnation of human hypocrisy, avarice, and selfishness. No one gets out clean—not even Bierce. For whom better to spread the word of evil than the Devil himself, the author of Bierce's eponymous work?

The Devil's Dictionary is a memoir of a man who knew all about selfishness and hypocrisy, a man who had seen hell. No wonder Bierce was adamant about the title. This was no T*he Cynic's t'Other*. This was a dictionary of the Devil.

There's a connection between the Devil and the word that goes back to the original Greek *diábolos*, which means "slanderer" or "accuser." Bierce knew all too well the demons that lurk in our language. He wrote that the cynic sees things as they are, but also wrote that they ought to be otherwise. This is another way of saying that the cynical writer's role is to bring the message of goodness. For only a writer who had known evil could channel virtue from the arms of the Devil and bring it back to humans. Bierce attacked goodness because he believed in it, not because he didn't. He attacked faith because he had lost it. It's notable that a definition for God is missing from T*he Devil's Dictionary*. It's as if Bierce was saying, anyone who wants to know about God should read the Bible, but anyone who wants to know humanity should read this.

***

> SATAN, n. One of the Creator's lamentable mistakes, repented in sashcloth and axes. Being instated as an archangel, Satan made himself multifariously objectionable and was finally expelled from Heaven. Halfway in his descent he paused, bent his head in thought a moment and at last went back. "There is one favor that I should like to ask," said he.
>
> "Name it."
>
> "Man, I understand, is about to be created. He will need laws."
>
> "What, wretch! you his appointed adversary, charged from the dawn of eternity with hatred of his soul — you ask for the right to make his laws?"
>
> "Pardon; what I have to ask is that he be permitted to make them himself."
>
> It was so ordered.

The archetypal Cynic is a 5th-century Greek fellow named Diogenes. He wasn't the only Cynic philosopher and he wasn't the first. But Diogenes' practice of Cynicism was so extreme, and so eccentric, that he came to define what we think of as classical Cynicism. Diogenes made fun of Alexander the Great and sabotaged the lectures of Plato. He was reported to dwell in a tub and live on a diet of onions. Diogenes is famous for stalking the streets of Athens carrying a lantern in the daytime, searching for an honest man (and infamous for masturbating in the marketplace). Diogenes, however, was no showboat. At the heart of Cynic philosophy was the message that virtue could only come through wisdom and self-sufficiency. The Cynic must be free of influence—wealth, power, fame, as well as social convention. In his antics, Diogenes was taking the word of Cynicism to its logical conclusion.

In this, Bierce walked in Diogenes' shoes. See, for instance, how Bierce's definition for SATAN fits comfortably with this tirade against the Greeks attributed to Diogenes:

> ...to all appearances you are men, you are apes at heart. You pretend to everything, but know nothing.... in contriving laws for yourselves you have allotted to yourselves the greatest and most pervasive delusion that issues from them, and you admit them as witnesses to your ingrained evil.

That people needed laws in the first place was evidence enough of their fundamental lack of virtue. The Cynic, thus, has no allegiances—no state, no home—for excellence cannot be attained when one pledges allegiance to institutions and traditions. Bierce, too, gave in to the dissolution of his family, his home, his allegiance to his country, his allegiance to anything save an impossibly high standard of moral virtue, which even he could not achieve. His rejection of the world was to the later detriment of his writing and, more important, his life, which ended as lonely as it began.

Two years after the publication of *The Devil's Dictionary*, Ambrose Bierce disappeared and never returned. He had gone on another one of his truth-seeking missions. Legend has it he traveled to Mexico and got caught up in Pancho Villa's revolution after making a tour of his old Civil War battlegrounds. Some say he met his end by firing squad, others say by his own hand. All we know is that, whatever he saw, Bierce never made it back to share the news.

Nobody knows what really happened to Bierce, but his definition of Heaven gives us a clue as to where Bierce might have hoped he'd end up.

> HEAVEN, n. A place where the wicked cease from troubling you with talk of their personal affairs, and the good listen with attention while you expound your own.

For Ambrose Bierce, this would have been Heaven indeed.

Stefany Anne Golberg

Sam Coppola and Joseph Ragno (Photo © Joan Marcus)

Godot

> "Perhaps he could dance first and think afterwards."
> Estragon, *Waiting For Godot*

One of the legends surrounding *Waiting For Godot*—and there are many, as is the case with all works of art that are mysterious and canonical—is that Samuel Beckett took his inspiration for the play from Caspar David Friedrich's *Man and Woman Observing the Moon.* The painting is quintessential Friedrich: a subject—in this case two—gazing solemnly out at the sublimity of Nature. The man and woman stand on a hill next to a craggy tree that is half-dead, uprooted, and leaning over a rock. The couple is wearing traditional German folk dress. They are motionless, transfixed by the sky, the moon, the ridge of pines in the distance. The man's arms are down; perhaps his hands are clasped before him. The woman keeps one arm at her side and her right hand rests gently on the shoulder of the man. "If there is one word for the mood of Friedrich's pictures it is 'longing'," wrote the critic Robert Hughes, "the desire, never satisfied, to escape from the secular conditions of life into union with a distant nature, to be absorbed in it, to become one with the Great Other, whether that other is a mountain crag, an ancient but enduring tree, the calm of a horizontal sea, or the stillness of a cloud."

Apparently, when someone once asked Friedrich what the couple was doing he replied, "These two are plotting some demagogic activities."

You can see the similarity to *Godot* at a glance: two lone figures in a desolate landscape, a craggy tree, the moon. In *Man and Woman Observing the Moon* the two figures face away from us, they face away from each other—they are faceless. Faces, for the man and woman, are unnecessary. They are *Rückenfiguren*, figures seen from the back. They can see themselves only in what they see outside of themselves. It is not necessary to speak about what they see; it is not even possible. What Friedrich paints is the ineffable. Before the great glory of Nature, man and woman are mute.

***

Vladimir and Estragon, the two main characters of *Waiting For Godot*, are anything but mute. The two men can hardly shut up. Each time they face a moment of silence, a moment of pause, they panic immediately, fall into despair, hold each other fast and talk some more.

In the course of the play, we come to know that these men have been friends for around fifty years, and that they were told—when and by whom we do not know—to wait by the tree in the moonlight for Godot. They are poor; we don't know why. As for Godot, we don't know what or who that is either, only that Vladimir and Estragon are desperate to meet him, that they have been waiting for an undetermined period of time, and that they will continue waiting. Or they won't. *Waiting For Godot* is not a play of answers. *Like Man and Woman Observing the Moon* it is a work of the ineffable, but an ineffableness very different than Friedrich's. As they wait for Godot, Vladimir and Estragon fill the void with nonstop activity. They talk about the past, talk about the future, talk about the Gospels, exchange shoes, exchange hats, talk with strangers, contemplate hanging themselves from the tree, feed each other, play act, pretend to be the tree, exercise, sleep, sing, contemplate the moon, contemplate leaving each other. Each time Vladimir and Estragon try to make sense of their situation, try to understand it, control it, reason with it, they are filled with anxiety. It is the attempt to understand that gets them in the most trouble. "What we know," says a character in Beckett's novel Watt, "partakes in no small measure of the nature of what has so happily been called the unutterable or ineffable, so that any attempt to utter or eff it is doomed to fail, doomed, doomed to fail. " Vladimir and Estragon don't know how to talk about anything without eventually being pointed to something unfathomable and inexplicable within their own selves. Every time they think they should know something, they talk and talk and talk and weep and cry until at last, dangling themselves over the abyss of the ineffable, they can only fall into an embrace.

ESTRAGON: Don't touch me! Don't question me! Don't speak to me! Stay with me!

VLADIMIR: Did I ever leave you?

ESTRAGON: You let me go.

> VLADIMIR: Look at me. (*Estragon does not raise his head. Violently.*) Will you look at me!
> *Estragon raises his head. They look long at each other, then suddenly embrace, clapping each other on the back. End of the embrace. Estragon, no longer supported, almost falls.*

About *Waiting For Godot* more has been written, considered, thought through, guessed at, and reasoned than possibly any play ever—at least any play in the last century. In writing about the ineffable, about the failure of knowing, Beckett opened up a whole can of speculative worms. People have guessed the play is about death. That it is about poverty. That it is about war. That it is about concentration camps. That it is about Christianity. That it is about waiting—whatever that means.

I remember well the first time I read *Waiting For Godot*. I felt, when I finished, that I had read a very great love story, maybe the greatest love story I had yet read. At that time I hadn't ever been in love, I was a teenager, but I felt all the hilarity and desperation in Vladimir and Estragon's predicament pointed to something profound between the men —a noisy and inexpressible disastrously inextricable love. Among all the crying and the fighting, all the vaudevillian rearranging of hats, the one thing Vladimir and Estragon cannot stop doing is loving. Even when they stop doing, they are still loving.

How did these two men find each other? Why do they stay together? Even they do not know. Or, at least, they cannot say. Love *is* the ineffable. Beckett understood this. Love transcends reason. What we can say about love, what we think we know about it, is reasoning after the fact. As Vladimir and Estragon wait for Godot they wait to know, they wait to be told what to do, what they are supposed to do, what they are supposed to know. In the meantime, they are loving. Estragon asks of Vladimir, "Who am I to tell my private nightmares to if I can't tell them to you?" And Vladimir says to Estragon, "You're my only hope."

When Beckett saw Friedrich's painting, and found inspiration for a play, he saw two figures with a deep longing, a never-satisfied desire. But whereas Friedrich expected his characters to find the sublime in (as Hughes put it) the Great Other, Beckett's characters—godless and rootless and filled with dread every time they look at the moon and the tree—find the sublime in the Other. Or rather, in each other.

"We should turn resolutely towards Nature," says Estragon to Vladimir. "We've tried that," replies Vladimir. "True," says Estragon. "Oh, it's not the worst, I know," says Vladimir. "What?" asks Estragon. "To have thought," says Vladimir. "Obviously," says Estragon. "But we could have done without it," says Vladimir. "*Que voulez-vous*?" asks Estragon. "I beg your pardon?" asks Vladimir. "*Que voulez-vous*," says Estragon. "*Ah! que voulez-vous*," says Vladimir. Exactly.

***

Vladimir and Estragon talk about escape. But they cannot. They are waiting for Godot. But why do they want to escape? And from what? From each other? To each other?

ESTRAGON: Oh yes, let's go far away from here.

VLADIMIR: We can't.

ESTRAGON: Why not?

VLADIMIR: We have to come back tomorrow.

ESTRAGON: What for?

VLADIMIR: To wait for Godot.

Do Vladimir and Estragon wish they could be finished? What would it mean if they stopped waiting for Godot? Each day of waiting means another day of loving, which means another day of wondering, of chatting, of surviving, of thinking, of knowing and not knowing. Of waiting.

When we say that love is ineffable, as Beckett knew, what we mean is that, when we love, we don't know what the hell we are doing. We can't stop talking through it, trying to figure it out. We think we ought to be talking about everything, doing everything, doing anything—breaking into spontaneous rage, talking about suicide, playing games, complaining about our boots—instead of just loving. We wait and wait and wait. Inevitably, boredom creeps in, terror creeps in. When you give yourself completely to another, as Vladimir and Estragon did, and you say, "Don't leave me, you're my only hope," every day is a little more and a little less frightening, every day is a little more and a little less suicidal, every day is a little more and a little less. You could, like Vladimir or Estragon, easily be talked into hanging yourself from a tree by the only one who could save you from it. We must escape. We cannot. We can't go on. We do.

"What's your name?" Pozzo asks Estragon in Act II. And Estragon replies, "Adam." Are Vladimir and Estragon Adam and Eve? Is their love just as primordial? Just as new?

Are all lovers Adam and Eve after the fall, wishing they knew whether they should keep on trying to get back to a prelapsarian state or move on?

> ESTRAGON: You'll help me?
>
> VLADIMIR: I will of course.
>
> ESTRAGON: We don't manage too badly, eh Didi, between the two of us?
>
> VLADIMIR: Yes yes. Come on, we'll try the left [boot] first.
>
> ESTRAGON: We always find something, eh Didi, to give us the impression we exist?
>
> VLADIMIR: (*impatiently*) Yes yes, we're magicians.

In love, Vladimir and Estragon make themselves and each other exist. They're magicians. But they also have the power to destroy. At one point, while they wait for Godot, Vladimir and Estragon decide to verbally abuse each other, just to distract themselves. Moron! Vermin! Abortion! Morpion! Sewer-rat! Curate! Cretin! Crritic! And then Estragon asks Vladimir, "Do you think God sees me?" as if only Vladimir would know.

Vladimir and Estragon are terrified by their love. They cannot trust it for an instant. One moment, they are in terror of losing it. Of losing themselves in it. Then, they believe in it again, and are happy. And it goes this way, on and on. From the very start of the play, this relentless dance of terror and elation is apparent. They don't trust each other. But they only trust each other. So there you are again, Vladimir says to Estragon, as if only he could know.

> VLADIMIR: So there you are again.
>
> ESTRAGON: Am I?
>
> VLADIMIR: I'm glad to see you back. I thought you were gone forever.
>
> ESTRAGON: Me too.
>
> VLADIMIR: Together again at last! We'll have to celebrate this. But how?

Maybe Vladimir and Estragon are terrified because they think they must know their love. And at the same time, they think that, if they figure it out, their love will no longer exist. They will no longer exist.

***

When we attempt to utter what we think know, Beckett wrote, we are doomed, doomed to fail. Trying to talk about love may be the most futile performance of all. But just because words fail love doesn't mean that love fails.

Samuel Beckett is not known for writing about love. But he was writing about love all the time. He wrote about love in his poem "Cascando":

> *why not merely the despaired of*
> *occasion of*
> *wordshed*
> *is it not better abort than be barren*
> *the hours after you are gone are so leaden*

they will always start dragging too soon
the grapples clawing blindly the bed of want
bringing up the bones the old loves
sockets filled once with eyes like yours
all always is it better too soon than never....

.....saying again
if you do not teach me I shall not learn
saying again there is a last
even of last times
last times of begging
last times of loving
of knowing not knowing pretending
a last even of last times of saying
if you do not love me I shall not be loved
if I do not love you I shall not love
the churn of stale words in the heart again
love love love thud of the old plunger
pestling the unalterable
whey of words
terrified again
of not loving
of loving and not you
of being loved and not by you
of knowing not knowing pretending
pretending....

Love love love thud knowing not knowing pretending pretending if you do not love me I shall not be loved if I do not love you I shall not love—this is the song of all lovers, the song of failing, of being doomed. Maybe we can be comforted by the fact that if we know we are failing, we also know we are loving. Just as Beckett saw in Friedrich's painting; that which is ineffable can be sublime.

VLADIMIR: You must be happy too, deep down, if you only knew it.

ESTRAGON: Happy about what?

VLADIMIR: To be back with me again.

ESTRAGON: Would you say so?

VLADIMIR: Say you are, even if it's not true.

ESTRAGON: What am I to say?

VLADIMIR: Say, I am happy.

ESTRAGON: I am happy.

VLADIMIR: So am I.

ESTRAGON: So am I.

VLADIMIR: We are happy.

ESTRAGON: We are happy. (*Silence.*) What do we do now, now that we are happy?

VLADIMIR: Wait for Godot.

A section from *Dulle Griet* by Pieter Breugel the Elder, 1563

Mad Meg

It's been 450 years since Pieter Breugel the Elder painted the famous *Dulle Griet*, and still no one can agree what the painting is about. In the center of the mad surreal landscape is Dulle Griet—in English 'Mad Meg'—a homely peasant woman from Flemish folklore, wearing the armor of a soldier. In her left hand she carries a cloth bag and a couple of baskets filled to spilling with kitchen items; tucked under her armpit is a small chest. In her free hand, she holds a long sword pointed at the mouth of Hell.

All around Dulle Griet, hellfires burn through the landscape, a city in ruin. There is an infestation of egg-shaped creatures. One such creature is dancing merrily on a burning rooftop in the background. In front of Dulle Griet is another egg-shaped creature with, I believe, a spoon inserted handle-first into its anus, which is also, possibly, its mouth. Behind Dulle Griet, an army of peasant women beat away invaders (demons? soldiers?). There's a story here, with a moral. There's always a moral amidst hellfire.

Most of what we know about Breugel comes from Carel van Mander, the 17th-century historian of Dutch art. In *Het Schilder-Boeck*, van Mander wrote of Breugel, "He made a

Dulle Griet, who is stealing something to take to Hell…" But some have translated this passage as "Dulle Griet who loots in front of Hell". Still others believe that Dulle Griet is preparing to pillage Hell itself for more booty.

The original religious interpretation of *Dulle Griet* is the one we broadly understand today: Dulle Griet is meant to be a denunciation of Greed. There is Dulle Griet with all her stuff, ready to pillage even Hell for more. Feminist interpreters have seen Dulle Griet as a depiction of male anxiety over what Simon Schama in *The Embarrassment of Riches* calls "the unmediated female" leading men into Hell with her "lust for shopping, a relish for malicious gossip, an uncontrollable temper, [and] unseemly cravings for rich, sweet food and strong drink." In Breugel's day, "Griet" was the name for a scolding, shrewish woman. Some say Dulle Griet is a personification of the Flemish proverb, "She could plunder in front of hell and remain unscathed." Your feelings about women in general will determine whether you think the proverb is a celebration or condemnation of female strength.

Bertold Brecht's Marxist appropriation of Dulle Griet for his Mother Courage kept Breugel's critique of Greed, but he turned Dulle Griet into a tragic heroine, a victim of capitalist warmongers (as well as her own iniquities). Set in 17th century, the play follows Mother Courage as she makes her way through war-torn Europe during the height of the Thirty Years' War. Like Dulle Griet, she is laden with stuff and carts her things across battlefields, determined to profit from the war that eventually takes her three children. In this interpretation, Dulle Griet is a failure both as a mother and as a profiteer. In other words, she is not only a bad woman but a bad robber.

***

You can see Bruegel's *Dulle Griet* at the Museum Mayer van den Bergh in Antwerp. I recommend going shortly after lunch, when the streets of Antwerp are at their busiest, though it has been five hundred years since you could call any street in Antwerp bustling. When I lived in Antwerp, in 2010, I made it a habit to visit the city's museums repeatedly and often. The Museum of Fritz Mayer van den Bergh was my favorite. Fritz Mayer van den Bergh was not himself an extraordinary man, nor even particularly artistic. He was born into a wealthy Flemish family in 1858 and was all set for a career in diplomacy when, in 1879, Mayer van den Bergh's father died, and van den Bergh decided that, after all, he did not want to work, in diplomacy or any profession. He was going to live with his mother. He would not marry and he would spend his time collecting art. He didn't really know anything about art, didn't befriend artists and collect their work like Guggenheim or Stein. But he pursued his occupation with great enthusiasm. When Mayer van den Bergh died suddenly in 1901 —fatally falling off a horse at age 43—his heartsick mother built a house in the center of Antwerp's banking district, and made it into a museum of her son's little art collection.

The existence of *Dulle Griet* at the museum is as much a point of pride as the surprising story behind its purchase. In 1897, Mayer van den Bergh saw *Dulle Griet* at an auction in Cologne. Only, he didn't know it was *Dulle Griet* and didn't know it was a Breugel. The painting's identity was unknown to all—the signature was illegible—and nobody was interested in buying the weird rendering of an armed woman approaching the mouth of Hell. But the painting suited the taste of Mayer van den Bergh just fine. He picked it up for about 500 francs, took it home, and a few days later, realized he had a bona fide masterpiece.

Everyone loves this kind of story. We all believe, a little, in life as a treasure hunt—for fortune, for love, for knowledge. But there is a secret to treasure hunting that only the real collector knows: To find real treasure is part luck, part accident, part "good eye", and a lifetime of sifting through crap. The crap-sifting, too, must be a genuine obsession. You must think of yourself as collecting all the time. You must become dedicated to the world of things.

Just picture yourself on a beach searching for shells. You always think you'll be satisfied with a single shell, but it is never so. You drift across the shoreline, picking bits of colorful broken pieces out of the sand and then hurtling them back. You may find one truly spectacular shell. But even this is rarely satisfying. If anything, the find makes your quest all the more urgent. It isn't long before you have slipped down the rabbit hole, into the quiet world of collecting. The shells become less important than the activity of searching for them. You can hardly hear the sound of the surf.

The real collector is pulled inexorably along on the path of collecting until he or she transcends the act itself. It is this process that, in part, makes the objects collected so very personal to the collector. Maybe this is why true collectors often become anti-social. Collectors can begin to develop an almost mystical relationship with "stuff". The need for everyday life fades. Collectors may find themselves, then, moving away from the world. They may find themselves moving toward Hell.

***

It's no accident that *Dulle Griet* looks like Hieronymous Bosch might have painted it. At the time Breugel was living and working in Antwerp, in the mid-16th century, the market for Bosch-type paintings was high. Breugel excelled at the style. Breugel also became well-known for paintings of simple Netherlandish peasants occupied with frolicking and fighting, and these too were popular with his patrons—wealthy businessmen and scholars who were, for their part, occupied with making Antwerp into the cosmopolitan capital of Europe. During Breugel's time, Antwerp was the center of European capitalism. It was a city defined by banking and international trade. The River Scheldt was lined with ships overflowing with merchandise from New Worlds. At the beginning of the 16th century, Antwerp accounted for 40% of world trade. It was New York City and Beijing all together. In his studio in Antwerp, Breugel painted scenes of country merrymaking and hay. But outside his window was the chaos and thrill of life during the Renaissance.

Behind the scenes of this metropolitan bustle was Europe as the theatre of battle and inquisition. The Thirty Years' War that was just on the horizon. Just seven years after Breugel's death, the Spanish would sack Antwerp for three bloody days—it would be the end of Antwerp's merriment. Throughout Breugel's life, the sacking and pillaging of towns and villages was routine business. In fact, it is believed that the mysterious journey of *Dulle Griet* from the Gallery of Rudolph II to its present home at the Museum Mayer van den Bergh in Antwerp began with the Swedish sacking of Prague in 1648.

One of Breugel's engravings, titled *The Battle Between the Money Bags and Strong Boxes*, was aptly described by Simon Schama as "capitalism as all-out war." Of course, Breugel was as dependent on the patronage of Antwerp's new rich as anyone. And yet, his paintings seem to condemn these very patrons, the men of leisure who pondered and danced as the villages of Europe burned. That is to say, Breugel condemned his own collectors, and also himself. Maybe *Dulle Griet* was painted to say, "We are all implicated in this unstoppable amassing of goods and fun. And it's got to stop somewhere."

***

There are two fascinating facts about Fritz Mayer van den Bergh: That he gave up a public career in diplomacy for the private pursuit of collecting things, and that he owned *Mad Meg*. For Fritz Mayer van den Bergh's desire to own *Mad Meg* seems as much a self-critique as Bruegel's desire to paint her.

There's another painting. This painting is called *The Bookworm*, painted by the German artist Carl Spitzweg in the mid-19th century. It is a painting of a man, standing on a library ladder. His wall of books surrounds him like a fort. The man's clothing is in disarray and he's got volumes stuffed in every crevasse of his person—in his right hand, under his left armpit, between his legs. In his left hand is also a book, it is open, and the man holds it right up to his nose. From the window, a ray of light illuminates this single open book, exaggerating the man's shortsightedness, which is both actual and metaphorical. Like Breugel before him, Spitzweg meant this painting as a critique of the collector, lost in his books, unable to look outside the window to the real world of war and politics (in this case, the period between the end of the Napoleonic Wars and the revolutions of 1848).

I mention this painting because it is one that Walter Benjamin draws attention to in his famous essay "Unpacking My Library". The essay—contrary to all the Breugels and Spitzwegs and Brechts even—is an enthusiastic defense of the collector. It is not just the thing collected that matters, Benjamin wrote—all the world comes alive to the collector engaged in the act of collecting. What a difference there is, he wrote, between the student who goes across the street to buy a textbook at a shop and the collector who goes across Europe on an acquisitional adventure. "Collectors are people with a tactical instinct," Benjamin wrote, "… the smallest antique shop can be a fortress, the most remote stationary store a key position." Nonetheless, the collector must always return to the den of things, where the collected items are appreciated. The things salvaged from remote stationary stores and dusty auction houses in Cologne must always have a private home with the collector.

> O bliss of the collector, bliss of the man of leisure! Of no one has less been expected, and no one has had a greater sense of well-being than the man who has been able to carry on his disreputable existence in the mask of Spitzweg's "Bookworm." For inside him there are spirits, or at least little genii, which have seen to it that for a collector —and I mean a real collector, a collector as he ought to be —ownership is the most intimate relationship that one can have to objects. Not that they come alive in him; it

> is he who lives in them. So I have erected one of his dwellings, with books as the building stones, before you, and now he is going to disappear inside, as is only fitting.

I wonder if anyone ever asked Fritz Mayer van den Bergh, the last collector of *Dulle Griet*, what he thought the painting meant. Perhaps the mouth of Hell looked to him as Benjamin describes his library, as a collector's dwelling, a haven for things. I wonder if van den Bergh didn't see himself in Dulle Griet, defending her possessions from the naysayers. Maybe, he thought, maybe Dulle Griet isn't a pillager at all but a collector, searching for a fortress to hold her stuff, and to come alive among the world of things. Perhaps the mouth of Hell is the only real option.

Stefany Anne Golberg

Soldier in Terracotta Army, Xian, China.

Two Weeks In China

May 7

6:49pm
"I was a Red Guard member in 1966, saw Our Great Leader Chairman Mao in Tiannanmen Square," Bill says with a big smile. "I tell you my life story, very sad. That's why I'm writing a book! About all my life experience. There's a picture of me in my Red Guard uniform during Cultural Revolution. I will show you!"

8pm
In the hotel room I turn on the television. On one channel there's a great battle scene from ancient times. On a second channel, a man in a suit sits behind a desk and angrily scolds another man with his pistol. A third channel shows a march of bloodied soldiers and filthy extras—men, women, children—dragging themselves down a dirt road. There's an elaborate Tang opera and an infomercial channel dedicated to selling products I can't identify. Hu Jintao addresses a congress and advertisements for the Beijing Olympics pop up regularly. On the one English-speaking

channel, Mongolians in folk costumes frolic through wide grassy fields. In the upper left-hand corner of most channels is a CCTV logo, the major state-run television broadcaster.

11pm
My mother meets me at the Jiangxian Grand Hotel in southern Beijing. She disappears into the elevator with her friend and I finish a late-night plate of bok choy in the empty Western-style restaurant, watching pink plastic lilypads bob in an artificial pond that overlooks the lobby.

May 8

4:30am
Neither my mother nor I can sleep. As she showers, there is a knock at the door. I throw on a robe and open it. A young man's hands are full of soap cakes and mini bottles of shampoo. He eyes me nervously and says nothing. I hold out my hands and he dumps all the soaps in them. I close the door and put the soaps on the TV. "Who was at the door?" my mother asks. "It was a man with soaps," I say. "I read that in China if you ask for something you get it immediately," she says. "Did you ask for soaps?" I ask. She pauses and turns to me. "No," she says, "I don't think so."

9am

China Daily: "CHINA SCENE", Thursday May 8, 2008

> Liu, a resident of Xinjin, Sichuan province, recently filed a lawsuit seeking child support payments from

his daughter…

Ma, an 18-year-old resident of Pingliang, Gansu province, kidnapped himself last Thursday in an attempt to extort money from his parents…

Hengxian county in Guangxi Zhuang autonomous region is enjoying a bumper jasmine harvest this year…

Guangzhou communities up to their neck in rats…

30 years after his death, the visage of Chairman Mao still watches over Tiananmen Square. But just behind him lie the empty, dusty rooms of concubines and the musty thrones of emperors. The gates that lead to the coiled dragons and ceremonial halls of the Forbidden City are flagged with boys who stand erect playing soldier. They are decorated with the red stars of the Communist Party. We are not allowed to take their picture. It is here that the story of the Empire's last days is told. Where the once-concubine Empress Cixi suddenly found herself caught in the middle of the 20th Century; on the one side, mustachioed foreigners who wanted to bring railroads and progress, on the other, armed Chinese traditionalists who wanted to punch the foreigners and their railroads back across the sea. For her part, Cixi simply wanted to keep her little Empire. It was what she knew. But she was smart, Cixi, she could see which way the wind was blowing.

Now, these rooms are visible only through the bits of streaky glass between the crowded heads of tourists.

12:35pm

A row of bicycle rickshaws carrying our tour group zips through the narrow hutong alleyways near the Bell and Drum Towers, part of an extensive complex of ancient planned residential areas. On the bus ride over, we see miles of walled-in scraps of hutongs that have been bulldozed in preparation for the Olympics, but we are told that our hutong area will be preserved as a national heritage site. Maybe we are driving in circles. We swerve through heaps of trash and ubiquitous laundry lines. A pair of women in their 50s or 60s sit on small stools by the side of the road, wearing jeans and red-and-yellow armbands. An old man in an army uniform and dark sunglasses sits cross-legged in front of a peeling doorway, a bamboo cane and sleeping dog at his feet. Locals in their 20s and 30s go about their day, repairing old windows, talking on cell phones, smoking. We're dropped in front of a traditional-looking home stuffed in the back of an alley which could be anywhere as far as we know. Inside, the middle-aged couple who live there serve us homemade dumplings, wok-fried things and beer. We are told that the traditional home is only a year old, that the government allowed the couple to build the new house with the agreement that they use it to feed tourists and show them the authentic dwellings of an average Chinese family. Most other buildings in this neighborhood are crooked and crumbling and have communal open-air bathrooms.

***

"What's China's national bird?
Cranes!"

***

4:01pm

Yellow cranes loom large in the grey skies of Beijing. Below them are shantytowns that house construction workers, bare barracks-style tents surrounded by the crumbling brick remnants of walls and homes. From the vantage of the Drum Tower in the north of the Inner City, I watch a shirtless man below washing his feet in a plastic bowl balanced on a pile of bricks. In front of his tent, an empty chip bag and a tin tea vessel. Bloated sky-high hotels and corporate centers are everywhere, standing over the razed remnants of ramshackle houses and apartments.

May 9

China Daily: "CHINA SCENE", Friday May 9, 2008

> Spurned lover spends her days wandering the streets...
>
> Fall after late-night trip to Net café leaves boy in coma...
>
> Starting this week, traffic police in Zhengzhou, capital of Henan province, will fine drivers who cover up license plates on vehicles used to fetch brides for wedding ceremonies. The fine will be 200 yuan ($29)...
>
> Starting this month, tour guides in Zhaoqing, Guangdong province, will no longer refer to their

> customers as "handsome boy" and "pretty girl". Instead, they will use tongzhi or "comrade". The goal is to improve services in the tourism industry...

8:31am

It's a bright spring day in Beijing.

On the grounds of the Temple of Heaven people kick around brightly colored hacky-sacks made of old tin and feathers. Below the bridge, scores of elderly Chinese sing songs praising Chairman Mao. Throughout the park, thousands of men and women twirl umbrellas, conduct slow-motion sword fights, line dance, do tai chi leg lifts, hop up and down, smile, smile, smile, for hours every morning, all in near-perfect synchronization. Music blares from boom boxes. An old man paints in quickly evaporating water on the concrete 'Hope Peace Longevity', and for us, 'Long Live Friendship Between Chinese and American People'.

4:30pm

The Great Wall of China, cloaked in fog and drizzle, surrounded by hills of green, cluttered with hundreds of giddy, giggling visitors from the world over, a rainbow of plastic ponchos and umbrellas, bumping into each other, falling down, squeezing through passages, hawking phlegm through parapets, in awe of their human achievements.

May 10

11:16am

The Tourists dislike squat toilets and are puzzled as to why we are eating so much Chinese food.

We arise each morning at the crack of dawn and proceed

with daily, brutal marches around the country, seeing its sights, speaking to no one. We have only each other. We walk through China behind a tattered pink flag unable to believe at times that we are in a real country and not some staged performance of a country.

8:14pm

Our bus drives down the main highway in the city of Xi'an at dusk. The road cuts through farmland topped with simple red brick residences. The streets are mostly empty, the buildings appear abandoned. A man pushes a wooden cart piled high with rags, a woman strolls far behind a newly walking baby. And then, as if the outskirts had all been a dream, the scene is replaced with row after row of stacks of apartment buildings, huge neon billboards, and sidewalks lined with late-night diners. Teenage boys play soccer in a field and I remember it is Saturday night in a medium-sized city of 8 million people. Amber, our cheerful young local guide says, if we want, we can call her Yang Yang.

May 11

11:16pm

In the market stalls that line Huajue Xiang alley next to the Xi'an Great Mosque middle-aged women in hijabs sell socks and Gucci knockoff purses. Young women in tight jeans sell fake antique opium pipes and call out in English. An outdoor chef stands behind an enormous wok atop a pile of flames, with skewers of raw pork neatly lined beside bowls of minced chilies and onions. A group of wrinkled hands spread bean paste and sesame seeds over a huge mass of thick white goo. It's Sunday.

3:30pm

Every day, an 80-year-old man who poses as the discoverer of the Terra Cotta Warriors sits in the Terra Cotta Warriors Museum gift shop to sign copies of the official Museum commemorative book in person. When Bill Clinton visited in 1998 to meet him and get his autograph, the Museum got an idea. And here he sits today, so delicate, as if a soft breeze would prove him to be a pile of dust in the shape of a man. He signs my book with a long, slow swoop, and I am overcome by a mob of Chinese teenagers clamoring for a signature of their own. Not long ago, you could get your picture taken with Mr. Yang. But the flash now hurts his eyes.

6:04pm

Mao wristwatches are plentiful in all the market stands. I think, at least a few of these merchants are old enough to remember the Great Leap Forward. Citizens made to melt down their cooking pots for the metal. People eating their own children. Deng Xiaoping's reforms in the 1970's led to what was effectually a denunciation of Maoism, and Mao's wife, and most things Mao. But Mao himself lives on, plastered to the sides of government buildings and on the wrists of foreigners.

6:30pm

This evening we are brought to the sprawling Grand Opera House Tang-Dynasty Palace, which, I suppose, is meant to resemble the palaces of the Tang Dynasty. Inside, foreigners are seated around lamp-lit tables, hunched over great piles of slippery dumplings. Before us, the grand stage stands empty.

Then the lights dim. Pretty women sway to prim folk music and swirl 10-foot-long sleeves that dangle from their arms. They remind me of fan-propelled tube puppets in front of car dealerships. Court dances of any nation are mincing steps and dreamy, fixed expressions. By the eighth act, suffering from dumpling exhaustion and sleeve hypnosis, the audience can no longer clap or move. Then, in Act 9, a man who makes quacking sounds with his face nearly brings the house down.

As I watch, a passage from a short story by Eileen Chang, the Chinese writer who died alone in her bare Los Angeles apartment, comes to mind:

> The furniture and the arrangement were basically Western, touched up with some unexceptionable Chinese bric-a-brac.... These Oriental touches had been put there, it was clear, for the benefit of foreigners...this was China as Westerners imagine it: exquisite, illogical, very entertaining.

May 12

2pm

Bill was raised in a poor mountainous village in Zhejiang province ("Where is Hangzhou you will go there"), the son of tea farmers. He was allowed to leave his village and attend university in 1964 but his studies were cut short in 1966 by the Cultural Revolution. "We went mad, you know, we went mad," he says over and over. He tells us he joined the youth militia and criticized the teachers he had gone to the city to learn from. He passes around his faded

Red Guard armband, laughing at it. He sings a song of Our Great Leader ("we went mad, you know, we went mad") and the bus driver joins in mechanically, paying more attention to the road. When Bill met his wife, she was a city girl in high school. Bill married her out of benevolence. She suffered in the country, we are told, though we're not given details. Then suddenly, the Cultural Revolution is over and things start to change. Mao dies, Mao's wife is arrested, and Bill's wife is allowed to escape the rural toil of farming life. She moves to the city and a few years later, in 1982—the government needing tour guides in the city as much as history teachers in the country—Bill and his son are allowed to join his wife, in the city where he resides today, still a tour guide at 64.

By the time Bill finishes his tale, half the bus is asleep with mouths gaping and eyes closed. A Canadian woman snores. Bill's real name is Huang.

From the spotty window, the farms of Hubei province whiz by. Eight people dressed in unremarkable clothes stand before a gravestone in what appears to be a random spot in a field. A trio of horn players point their brass instruments into the blazing sun, their song silent from the tour bus.

6pm

Aboard the M.V. Emperor, where we will spend the next four days, we are assaulted by a long line of grinning uniformed crew members. Two haggard men in ripped t-shirts stumble into the crowd. They carry a load of heavy suitcases that dangle from a bamboo stick balanced on their shoulders. Among the tourists, there is a collective gasp and nervous giggling. They deposit the bags heavily. Someone fumbles around in her pocket for a yuan or two. But the crooked men have already left.

May 13

6:53am

The peagreen Yangtze moves beneath us as we set sail upstream. The river is dotted with small pointy fishing boats. Brick shacks peek out between the trees that cover the surrounding high mountains. The air is alive with tiny white butterflies. You've seen it in pictures: the mist, the cliffs—it hasn't changed for a while or so it seems. But the Yangtze is indeed is changing, it's just that much of the past is already far beneath the surface.

8am

Our first breakfast on the ship is what has now become my daily morning fare: congee (white, black, corn, millet) topped with spicy pickled things. It is the only item that never seems to run out at the breakfast buffet. "There was some sort of earthquake yesterday," a woman says.

9:30am

Largest Project
Enormous Benefit
Solves Longstanding Problems
Inheritance Civilization
Most Attractive Sightseeing

Our ship docks and the bus takes us through the port town of Sandouping. Babies with open bottom flaps mooning our tour bus, a woman frying egg pancakes in a 10-gallon pan, dogs eating alley trash, old men crouched on tiny bench seats playing cards—all by the early light of morning.

We wind through camphor and orange trees to the Three Gorges Dam Project, the largest dam in the world. Our daily guide shoots facts and figures at the group, assuring us that, though the Project will eventually displace well over a million people, he received an apartment much nicer than his previous one. We're dropped in the middle of a tidy park that plays orchestral music straight from a '30s love scene.

> ...the whole Yangtze Three Gorges has a crashing change, it become to be a huge artificial lake....The Three Gorges Project is the dream that makes our country stronger, but when the dream comes true, our old but beautiful hometowns also become a parting old dream. It is unavailable to be satisfied for the both sides in the world....Losing some beauty of seclusion and grotesque, the Three Gorges increases some magnificence...Good wishes for the Three Gorges!
> *—Lu Jin, Chief Editor, "Three Gorges Project in China", February 2008*

An island of tall white apartment buildings looms on the horizon, new homes for the displaced villagers whose old homes were devoured by the Dam.

Back down in the park, I buy a government-issued book about the Dam. Next to me, a man plays a creaky 'My Darling Clementine' over and over on the hulusi.

Oh my darlin'
Oh my darlin'
Oh my darlin', Clementine

You are lost and gone forever
Dreadful sorry, Clementine

9:30pm

The ship's crew has prepared a talent show. The performances are amateurish and sincere. The bartender kicks her legs in the air. The waitress who giggles stays at the back, giggling. There are more floppy sleeve dances and also a Mexican hat dance of sorts. No one has much information about the earthquake in Sichuan province. 10,000 dead we hear.

Later, I ask Bill which, in his opinion, had a greater effect on China's economic liberalization, the death of Mao or the 1976 earthquake in Tangshan that killed 250,000 people. He stares at me straight-faced for a moment then starts to laugh loudly. "Ah! Good one, good one!" he says.

May 14

9:46am

The 2,000-year-old village of Dachang in Wushan County is under water. Our boat guides today again tell us about their new, better homes on top of the hill. Cherry shows us pictures from a book called 'Charming Wushan'. The photos of the pre-submerged Dachang show a windy place with traditional Chinese rooftops. In Dachang, Cherry shared a tiny apartment with her husband, daughter, and parents-in-law. Their outdoor toilet was shared with four other neighboring families. The new Wushan in the picture book is a round and gleaming Tomorrow World. From the boat, it looks like the same white concrete, laundry-dappled blocks one sees all over China. Cherry's new apartment in the Wonder City, she tells us, has indoor plumbing, cable, and internet access. For 50,000 yuan, Cherry was able to buy her apartment outright from the government. She has multiple rooms and her daughter loves to read on the john, sometimes for 45 minutes. Cherry's in-laws never made the move to new Wushan. Both died shortly after being told of the imminent relocation. Cherry says they were too old to make the change.

Our boat drifts past a tiny farming island sprinkled with cornstalks and a few shacks that frame three women folding laundry. The shacks sit casually by a handful of 3,000-year-old graves, holes carved in the side of the hill with small wooden coffins peeking out. Next year, it too will be sunk.

We transfer to a small motorized sampan boat to explore the nooks of the Lesser Three Gorges. Suddenly, a Tujia man who has been sitting next to me in the sampan rises. He wears pinstripe trousers and dons a traditional straw lid, and as he stands he belts out a warbling, sonorous melody. Above us, the dark mouths of caves built to shelter the locals from Japanese airstrikes during the Second World War.

Ruby lips above the water
blowing bubbles soft and fine
but alas I was no swimmer
so I lost my Clementine.

May 15

11am

Just outside the City of Ghosts a man with mirrored sunglasses and faded jeans leans on a crooked bamboo stick in front of a one-room police station. His head is turned to the right but he watches nothing. A Double Happiness cigarette dangles from his mouth.

Apparently, Chinese Hell is just another round of bureaucracy. You must obtain a travel permit simply to pass through Hell's Gate and then endure interrogation by the officials of Hell. They will judge if you are to return to earth a human again or be tortured for your sins before your next life as a beast of burden. Staying dead is not an option.

6,000 steps. Up up up, past the Ridge of Helplessness, the Balcony of Nostalgia, Nothing-To-Be-Done Bridge, and Last-Glance at Home Tower, where the dead can have a final look at the world. Pushed ever upwards we are wedged into the Palace of the King of Hell. Behind an old gate, miniature model scenes of what the torture chambers in the Chinese underworld might have in store.

The Palace of the King of Hell is the only original structure left in the City of Ghosts. Everything else was built in the 80s. Officially, there is no answer as to why this particular building was left intact while the surrounding temples were laid waste. But it is agreed, at least in Fendgu, that the Red Guards who blazed through here knew as well as anyone that the Kingdom of Hell is a place of judgment, where crimes are punished without mercy and you can never escape your sins.

4:16pm

Sailing westward, once you pass the Gorges, the banks of the Yangtze change. The scene is an endless succession of enormous grey concrete factories and rusty barges hauling coal or trucks. Gone are the warbling birdsong and the towering limestone peaks. The new song of the Yangtze clanks and grinds. Makeshift docks curve up hills into processing plants painted with filth and haze. A lone fisherman in an aluminum canoe drags the afternoon carp from the brown river water. In the distance, I can make out a row of workers in red shirts ("red in China means good luck!") filing into a lopsided tent perched on a mile-long rock pile. We pass under bridge after bridge, some of them just long lengths of filament strung high over the water that sway as workers stumble across carrying heavy loads on sticks.

Up on the sundeck, the sun is an impressionistic smudge. Unable to breath comfortably outside, most of the tourists have chosen to stay in their rooms. I awake each morning my throat thick with phlegm and I haven't yet learned the popular art of Chinese hawking.

"Here it is," said Tocqueville of 19th-century Manchester, once the world's factory, "that humanity achieves for itself both perfection and brutalization, that civilization produces its wonders, and that civilized man becomes again almost a savage."

9:30pm

It's the last night of the cruise. By the light of the dull Yangtze moon, I write a note to the maid:

> Dear Amenda,
>
> Thank you so much for your lovely notes. I was particularly touched by the little paper heart you left and the drawing of Garfield (the cat). I wonder how long it takes you to handwrite these notes every day. I don't know you at all but I will keep your notes and take them back with me to New York, and they will be a memory of you. Hopefully you will under-

stand this or someone will translate it for you. I wish you the very best of luck.

Warm wishes,
Stefany Anne Golberg
Room 218

On to Chongqing.

May 16

7:11am
Chongqing smells like an old nail.
I stand on the dock where the M.V. Emperor has left us for good. My contact lenses stick to my eyeballs.
"It's a bit…polluted," I say to our Chongqing guide, a university professor who drags tour groups around on off hours.
"You mean, the air?" he says.
"Well, yes," I say. We walk on towards our bus.
"And, the water?" he says.
"Yes, that too."

1:30pm
Tin-roofed mud-and-brick homes are built into the side of the Chongqing hills overlooking the river. Long strips of meat dangle over porch railings and windowsills to dry in the sun. Along the river highway, rows of dank WWII air raid shelters have become a makeshift market, selling scrap metal, car parts, and broken bits of stuff, the remnants of Chongqing as wartime capital.

11:46pm

The businessmen in the lobby of the Royal Plaza Hong Kong Hotel drink frothy fruity cocktails and watch the live music with glazed attention. An expressionless woman in skinny black leggings sings “I’d Like To Make it With You”. Behind them, two screens show a soccer game and the Fashion Channel. Upstairs in my room, I flip through one grisly earthquake scene after another on CCTV. The soap operas have been suspended. Instead, children pulled from masses of rubble, entire villages flattened by shoddy building and bad timing. A schoolyard becomes a waystation for corpses. Day after day parents wait in the yard for new bodies, waiting to see if it is their missing child, their only child.

May 17

11:22am

Atop the lush Victoria Peak, the crown of British colonialism in Hong Kong, a bathroom attendant stands at attention with one hand gloved in black latex, the other holding a pair of salad tongs to fish discarded toilet paper from the waste bin.

May 18

9:25am

Our train flies along the path from Hong Kong to Guangzhou. Wall-less, tin-roofed farmer’s shacks are planted in the lush vegetation of Guangdong Province. All around them, half-finished (or half-demolished) modern apartment complexes are caged in rickety bamboo scaffolding.

China is growing everything. More apples than America, more chilies than Mexico. Child-sized palm fronds shelter mounds of smoldering garbage.

2:01pm

"There's only one landlord in China," says Hobbie, "the Party." You may own your own home, he tells us, but you'll never own the earth beneath. Hobbie speaks English like Queen Elizabeth. "Guangzhou is very international," he says, "you will see blacks." Rather than leading us single file behind a flag, Hobbie cuts us loose into a seething pit of shopping exuberance. Locals scrabble for jeans, tops, dresses, cheap glass baubles shaped like rats and pigs and oxen, jade-colored cigarette holders. Shopgirls stand high in the middle of clothing bins, throwing discount items to teenagers who push each other to snap them up. A teenage boy wears a t-shirt that says, "I Do What I Want To Do". One woman's shirt just says BALLS.

May 19

10am

In *Marco Polo and His Travels*, Polo declared Hangzhou to be the finest and noblest city in the world. Hangzhou is a mirage that floats above the rest of the country. The air is shiny, the people are shiny, the emerald tea plantations spiral up into the mist. Even our local tour guide Ricky is much crisper and peppier than our previous ones. Along the West Lake, sunny Hangzhou children wear heart-shaped stickers of the national flag and hold their fingers in a 'V for Victory' sign.

2:28pm

Our bus driver pulls over to get gas and a handful of cars and trucks start to honk. We can't figure it out. The honks don't seem to be directed towards anything in particular. Should we be honking? I try to locate our driver and see him filling the tank and having a smoke. "Oh!" says Bill. "It's the mourning! The mourning! Three days of mourning for the earthquake." Not knowing what day it is, having had spotty access to news sources, we put together that it's the exact moment the earthquake had hit one week earlier —2:28pm, May 12—when we were on a bus listening to Bill tell us his life story. And that's how we found ourselves on the first day of a countrywide moment of unity for the earthquake victims—on the side of a highway, oblivious, surrounded by a few pitiful and patriotic toots, pointed towards Shanghai.

3pm

Huge new houses line the Huhang Expressway. They're topped with shiny silver cupolas that reach toward heaven. These are the homes of the upgraded Chinese farmer. They are the countryside turned suburb. The farmers here can cultivate anything they want, so long as it's a cash crop, like silk pods, which are a lot more profitable than rice. Some will also take jobs in one of the many factories that line the outskirts of Shanghai, further increasing their income. The Tourists are impressed; these homes are far larger than anything they live in.

Bill dismisses our surprise by telling us that the homes were built on the cheap. Then he excitedly points out a lake where the Communist Party was founded in 1921 and recites a list of Chinese names that we can't understand and will never remember.

***

"CHARM SHANGHAI IS SPLENDID DAILY"

***

9pm

The City of Lights' City of Lights is dim. Tonight—and for the next two nights—China flies at half-mast to honor the earthquake dead. At 9pm the television stations play either earthquake news or silent snow. The Tourists are disappointed because we cannot watch the Shanghai Acrobats as scheduled. There are no public entertainments anywhere, in all of China.

On a street corner in Shanghai, a group of young people anxiously hold out Styrofoam containers to a man who flips fresh noodles around in a fire-heated wok. Ladies get coifed in open-air salons. Across the way, a gym displays a row of late-night exercisers. There's one bar open and it's empty except for a pair of middle-aged Chinese men silently drinking green tea from a glass pot. I order a Shanghai Night and get served a Long Island Iced Tea. Monday night life is performed, a wordless mime. Shanghai continues, only in darkness.

May 20

9:33am

Back on the bus someone asks Ricky about Falun Gong. He laughs. They laugh. But, what is Falun Gong? someone asks, laughing. Ricky laughs. Bill laughs. Everyone laughs. Falun Gong is taboo, Ricky says, laughing. But no, really, a few more tourists pipe in, laughing, can you explain Falun Gong to us? Because we see stuff about it in the States but we don't understand what the big deal is. Bill and Ricky laugh. The Tourists start to speak to each other ("Do you know what it is?" "Do you?"). Bill and Ricky have turned away, and have stopped laughing.

2:15pm

Everything we do, every place we go—every hotel we stay at, every restaurant, garden, every attraction and splendid site—has been officially sanctioned by the PRC government. No one tells us this, but it is obvious. Any request for a change in itinerary is met with a dismissive grin. By the end of Week Two, I have taken to sneaking away from prescribed visits to tourist factories. I find myself on unremarkable streets, locals-only districts where workers eat noodles on twist-tied scaffolding and the shops are mostly empty. Daily life waltzes along to the music of whining drills. I can't speak to anyone, people watch me with confusion. Why am I here, the faces ask, in this neighborhood, on this street?

May 21

Li Po, the great Tang-era poet, spent most of his life wandering around China. His poems are traveler's reflections, but really they tell the story of Li Po himself, the lone poet vagabond, a tourist in his own country. His average was "a hundred poems per gallon of liquor" and the poems have titles like 'Alone Looking At The Mountain', 'Alone And

Drinking Under The Moon', 'Looking For A Monk And Not Finding Him', 'Drinking Alone'.

Li Po traveled because he couldn't find a place to settle in. A constant traveler, he was forever homeless, and the journey became his home.

Li Po, so they say, drowned in the Yangtze when he fell out of his boat in a drunken attempt to embrace the reflection of the faraway moon, perhaps thinking that it was his next destination. And, maybe it was.

Quiet Night Thoughts

Before my bed
there is bright moonlight
So that it seems
Like frost on the ground:

Lifting my head
I watch the bright moon,
Lowering my head
I dream that I'm home
—Li Po

It's sunny today in Shanghai. The streets are paved with dried magnolia petals and construction rubble.

Dancing Mania in the Middle Ages (unattributed)

Hysteria

First, there was dancing. They say it started somewhere in Europe, some time in the 7th century. They danced one Christmas in Bernberg but there is nothing so unusual about that. In 1237 a group of children danced from Erfurt to Arnstadt, and forty-one years later two hundred people danced on the bridge spanning the River Meuse, until the bridge collapsed, and they all fell in.

It happened again one day in 1374, in the German town of Aachen, and the dancing lasted for three hundred years more. In late June, the streets of Aachen erupted with wild, mad dancing that nobody could explain. The dancers twisted their bodies around and shook and frothed at the mouth. They saw things that others could not see, they laughed until they screamed. For three hundred years the Western side of the continent of Europe was terrorized by dancing like this. The dancers were not special. They were just regular people inexplicably seized with dancing. Any ordinary French or German or English or Flemish person could become a dancer at any moment, and you never knew when dancing could strike. Dancers danced until they lost their breath and collapsed, until they lost themselves, until they starved. They shook and moaned and made animal sounds and wept and ripped off their clothing. Some thought the dancers unholy, demonic, supernatural, possessed.

The dancing mania reached its peak in the early 16th century. In Strasbourg, in July of 1518, Frau Troffea had an irresistible desire to dance. She went into the streets and began to dance and didn't stop for days. She danced for a week as scores of Strasbourgians watched her, and then they too got the urge. They danced and danced for three weeks more until their number became a hundred. At this point the authorities of Strasbourg intervened. They announced that the dancers would be forced to dance without stopping until they were cured. Guildhalls were set aside to make room for the dancers, a stage was built, and professional musicians were hired. The pipes and drums encouraged the dancers to dance all the more wildly. Within days of this carnival, the weakest dancers were dead. By the end of August about four hundred citizens of Strasbourg had been cursed with the dancing plague. They danced until they were ecstatic and then they started to die. The dancers fell to the ground exhausted, suffering heart attacks and strokes. The survivors were loaded into a wagon and driven to a local shrine. Everyone begged the saints to be healed of the unstoppable dancing.

By the middle of the 17th century, the dancing had stopped. To this day, no one can agree on its cause. Some say it must have been something the dancers ate—food poisoning maybe—or maybe some dancers had epilepsy or typhus, though this could not be an explanation for everyone. Others say that the dancing happened during times of hardship, that the dancers were just stressed out. They believed they were being punished by angry spirits and danced to alleviate their fear.

It's true that the dancers were mostly peasants and poor, sometimes dreadfully poor and sometimes starving. Famine and disease and war were just the way of things for European peasants in the Middle Ages. Maybe peasants turned to dancing the same way others turned to prayer. Some say the dancing stopped in the 17th century because the Protestant Reformation extinguished the sense of the supernatural among the peasants of Europe.

But these days, everyone seems to agree that dancing mania was a "collective hysterical disorder"—that the dancers went mad together. For hundreds of years, now and then, a collective madness would sweep through the towns of Europe. Nobody knew why it happened and nobody could make it stop. It would end only when it wanted to, when the dancing had reached full frenzy.

Though their method seems rather cruel, perhaps the authorities of Strasbourg were right. Allowing the dancing to culminate in ecstasy seemed the only way the mania would end. The other two choices seemed to be death, or return to ordinary life.

***

Later, there was paralysis. It was most extreme in the second half of the 19th century and lasted into the early 20th. Men and women in Europe, and in America too, found that they could not move. Their limbs went dead and their eyes went blank—their bodies would not obey them. Incidents of muteness became increasingly prevalent. People suddenly lost the power of speech, or they went deaf, or lost their sense of taste or smell. Some people would walk about as if in a trance and later remembered nothing. Others would fall asleep and sleep for days; these people appeared to be dead. Doctors were baffled by the phenomenon and did not know what to do. They relieved these immobilized people of their dead limbs and blind eyes and hoped it would be helpful.

And then the new study of psychology pronounced the paralyzed "hysterical," though the term was, admittedly, broad. The hysterical symptoms, the psychologists said, were manifestations of an abnormal psychological state. It was agreed that, though hysterical people were just ordinary people, they were people who could not live ordinarily. Sigmund Freud wrote that hysterics turned away from reality because they found reality unbearable. The psychologist Pierre Janet went further. He wrote that hysterics had lost the function of reality altogether. But after all, wrote Pierre Janet, such people have something to teach us:

> There have always been strange persons who raised the admiration of the crowd because their nature seemed to be different from human nature. Their manner of thinking was not the same as that of others; they also had extraordinary oblivions or remembrances, they had visions, they saw or heard what others could not see or hear. They were illumined by odd convictions; not only did they think but they also felt in another way than the bulk of mankind; they had an extraordinary delicacy of certain senses joined to extravagant insensibilities which enabled them to bear the most dreadful tortures with indifference or even with delight. Not only did they feel but they also lived otherwise than other people; they could do without sleep, or sleep for months together;

> they lived without eating or drinking, without satisfying their natural needs.
>
> ....Well, all these phenomena, as you know already, are the usual symptoms of hysteria, and there is not, from this point of view, a disease which has played so great a part in history. If I am not mistaken, it is still exactly the same now: we have changed only in appearance...every time we want to throw some light on the mysteries of our destiny, to penetrate into the unknown faculties of the human mind, to whom do we appeal? Whom do we take as a subject of observation? Is it an ordinary person, a person in good health, whom we ask to foresee the future or to talk with the dead? No; it is a neuropathic patient, insensible to the things of this world, but whose sensibility is overexcited in a certain direction; medically speaking, it is a hysteric person.

Like the mad dancers, it's possible that hysterics lost control over their bodies when they lost control of their lives. Their paralysis was, perhaps, a protest over the powerlessness of everyday life. But Pierre Janet was making a point far more powerful than this. The loss of the function of reality, Janet was saying, was a kind of ecstatic experience. Hysterical paralysis was an ecstasy of silence and stillness, but it was an ecstasy nonetheless. Hysteria was a desire for extraordinary oblivion.

***

There were the African laughers and the French wanderers and the nuns who mewed like cats. There were the 19th century young women in the English servant class who suffered a pandemic of ulcers. In 1983 a thousand Palestinian girls fainted. In 1967, in Singapore, over a thousand men used clamps and pegs to stop their genitals from disappearing.

***

Then came the allergies. The very sight of flowers would send people into fits of sneezing. Millions in the late 20th century were allergic to animals and plants—just the air made them sick. Air was clouded with mold and dust and pollen and terrifying, invisible particles. The skin of the allergic became hypersensitive to everything they touched. Ordinary food was intolerable. Then came asthma, the phenomenon of mass breathlessness, which has increased globally by fifty percent every decade for the past forty years. Four thousand people in England each year are told they can no longer eat peanuts. In the United States intolerance to gluten has quadrupled in just fifty years.

These afflictions were called autoimmune diseases, though no one was quite sure what that meant. Otherwise normal people with autoimmune diseases were mysterious and incurable. The bodies of people with autoimmune diseases seemed to be attacking themselves.

Then came the back pain and the repetitive stress disorders and the migraines and pains with no names. Excruciating pain seemed to make sense, perhaps, for a field or factory worker. But the vast majority of pain sufferers did not have physically taxing lives. People would throw their backs out tying their shoes or hurt themselves while sitting. Some would awake from sleep in the morning to find that they were crippled. The physical ailments were given the name chronic pain. The name was frightening. It meant that the pain had no cause and could not be cured and, moreover, would go on forever.

In our time, millions claim to have experienced at least one chronic ailment—some have experienced them all. Average people who seem otherwise healthy become incurably and hopelessly sick. They stop going to work, stop eating and sitting and traveling like other people. They live long lives full of medicine and canes and pills and rules. They live like they are dying.

But when we want to see into the unknown faculties of the human mind, asked Janet, to whom do we appeal? The dancing sneezing maniac comes to us as a beacon, shining light on the mysteries of our destiny. The hysterical person, illumined by odd convictions, enduring tortures others cannot. The hysterical person, who loses the function of reality in the hope it can be found again.

"And the dance mania found its own way through time to survive among us," wrote the poet Jonathan Aaron, "as untouched as ever by the wisdom of science."

Think of the strange, magnetic sleep
whole populations fall into every day,
in gymnasiums full of pounding darkness,
in the ballrooms of exclusive hotels,
on verandahs overlooking the ocean and played upon
by moonlight, in backyards, on the perfect lawns
of great estates, on city rooftops, in any brief field
the passing tourist sees as empty—
how many millions of us now, the living
and the dead, hand in hand as always,
approaching the brink of the millennium.

Kate and Maggie Fox (circa 1850), Moravia New York

Moravia

And just like that, America was haunted. When exactly the apparitions began appearing no one could say for sure. It was the middle of the 19th century—maybe 1848? This was the year that the young Fox sisters, Maggie and Kate, began communicating with the ghost of a murdered man who had been buried in the cellar of their new house in Hydesville, New York. The girls listened to his frantic rappings beneath the floorboards and created a Morse code of sorts to parse the meaning. Their mother called in the neighbors to witness her daughters' supernatural powers and the neighbors' excited whispers stretched to surrounding towns. They particularly excited Amy and Isaac Post, a progressive Quaker couple who were friends of the Fox family. The Posts relocated Kate and Maggie to their home in Rochester and soon the girls were performing séances for the Posts' reformist friends. Strangely, the rappings followed them all the way there. The Rochester rappings became known all over the country, talked about by William Cullen Bryant and P.T. Barnum and Mary Todd Lincoln. The Fox sisters—now famous mediums—had started a movement. They were just twelve and fifteen years old.

Or, the hauntings could have started the year that Mary Andrews began conducting séances from her house on Oak Hill Road in the western New York village of Moravia. Her nightly spirit conjurings drew thousands to Moravia—the hotels there were always full, despite being haunted too. In 1872 Mary Todd Lincoln came to the house on Oak Hill Road, searching for her own ghosts. These famous events turned Moravia and the nearby city of Auburn, a new city built on the wealth of the Erie Canal, into the Mecca of the Spiritualist movement. From there, the ghosts would spread. They would appear in familiar haunts all across the country: overlarge hotels, moldering basements, the salons of the rich.

Mediums will tell you that the ghosts are always there, that we the living share this earth with the dead. Sometimes the dead can be called from the underworld and invited to join us for tea. But some restless souls get stuck between heaven and earth, they don't know how to go home. Their despair lingers in dark closets and they appear to the living when their restlessness is strong. This is what 'apparition' means. It is an appearance, a revelation of something already there. And every so often, a living person who is extra perceptive—often a child and usually female—becomes a breathing channel for spirits, a voice for the voiceless, a bridge between life and mystery, a bridge between now and then.

For some reason, the spirits started appearing in the middle of the 19th century and mostly around Seneca Lake in western New York. For thousands of years after Ice Age glaciers melted into finger-shaped lakes, this small part of the world was mostly filled with animals and people living out in the green. In the 18th century genocide arrived in the

Finger Lakes, in the guise of an American General named Sullivan whose job it was to destroy all the villages of the Native Americans living there. American settlers showed up soon after to build humble cabins and live modestly upon the graves of the Iroquois. They lived there invisibly for twenty-odd years, just hours from New York City, until one day in 1825, they looked into their fields and realized an enormous canal had been carved into the hills. Not long after its completion, the builders of the canal decided that it wasn't enormous enough. So, in the 1840s the Erie Canal was carved deeper and wider and busier and louder. Steamships and industry roared over farms, turning villages into towns and cabins into mansions.

The Erie Canal became an information superhighway that carried the ideas of progress all around New York State. As industrialists sipped whiskey on their brand-new verandas, runaway slaves traversed an underground city below them. Frederick Douglass sat in the back of the Wesleyan Chapel in Seneca Falls at the First Women's Rights Convention, listening to Elizabeth Cady Stanton and Lucretia Mott and diligently taking notes. A few miles down in Auburn, the home of Harriet Tubman became a haven for fugitive family and friends escaping slavery. Hicksite Quakers in Rochester called for a boycott of slave-made products and preached radical nonresistance. A bit further east, the Oneidists created a Communalist Utopia. They promoted free love and equality and believed they were living in heaven on earth. The whole region was inflamed by utopianism and religious revivals and Pentecostals preaching the Second Great Awakening. William Miller predicted Jesus would surface in upstate New York around 1843, and when Jesus failed to show, his disappointed Millerite congregation became the Seventh Day Adventists instead. Up in Palmyra, a teenage farm boy named Joseph Smith was utterly overwhelmed by all the Protestant sects blazing through his community—he couldn't make up his mind which to choose. Then, he had a vision for an entirely new religion that was shown to him by an angel. Thus was Mormonism born. In 1876, Charles Grandison Finney called this region of western New York "Burnt-over" because by then there was no one left to convert. The region drew reformers from Boston and Washington, D.C. and Philadelphia—it was the place to be. As fast as you can imagine, upstate New York was not just part of the story of American progress. It was the story of American progress.

This is all to say that antebellum northeastern America was spiritually itchy. Prevailing theologies were insufficient to those who were looking for relief. Many established churches had little to say when it came to women's rights and ending slavery. And then there were the ghosts. The more people talked about them the more ghosts appeared, and word of the hauntings ran the length of the Canal. Hardboiled journalists and famous scientists poured into the region by the boatload. They came ready to debunk and denounce. Frederick Douglass—a good friend of the abolitionist Posts, visited Rochester in 1850. He listened to the rappings, he later wrote in the North Star, and was respectfully unconvinced that their source was "unearthly." But more often than not, people came as skeptics and left as true believers. The legendary newspaper editor Horace Greeley was fascinated by Spiritualism—for a time the Fox sisters lived in his home. The spirits and their mediums were increasingly invited to dinner parties thrown by progressive elites. In these circles, séances were no mere party game, "midnight fumblings over mahogany" as Emerson sneered. Communing with the dead was part of the mystical revolution.

The tenets of Spiritualism were an assortment of ideas taken from the somewhat messier domains of the Enlightenment. These ideas were merged with the reformist ideas of the day. Spiritualists talked about Emmanuel Swedenborg, about the spongy boundaries between the material and cosmic worlds, about the individual's inner core of divinity. They talked of the philosopher Charles Fourier, who wrote of a new world order based upon a universal harmony. They wrote of the experiments of the physician and arts patron Franz Anton Mesmer, who believed in an interconnectedness between all the heavenly bodies and natural life forms, that energy moved from the planets to the human body and could be passed from one body to another through this universal force. To say you were a Fourierist communitarian and a feminist and maybe a Transcendentalist and an abolitionist and a Spiritualist was stylish and understood. It all boiled down to one basic understanding: That Americans were little parts of a greater social-spiritual whole, that all people were a unified species to be organized in a perfect fellowship, as Henry James would say.

This points to an important fact of Spiritualism. It's not that Spiritualists were the only Americans who believed in ghosts. Americans have historically been, more often than not, believers. It's not that people in the South, or African Americans, or Native Americans were less inclined to the supernatural. There was a reason why the ghosts all seemed to be gathered in the North. Spiritualism was transcendence for white antebellum intellectuals.

When we talk about a place being haunted—even if we do not believe in spirits and we are speaking only in metaphors – we are talking about the present being disturbed by the past. The "spirit" of the past comes knocking on our door and reminds us that we are not alone, lone actors in the land of now, unwatched by the dead actors of history. America in the mid-19th century was everything she set out to be—independent and wealthy, a country at peace, a civilized land whose borders were still mythic and wild. The heroic story of America had been written, and yet her citizens were panicked. Somehow the story couldn't end just there, it didn't feel quite right.

Spiritualists fit weirdly in the story of America, less because of what Spiritualists believed than who the Spiritualists were: physicians, scientists, writers, politicians, industrialists—white, prominent, educated, wealthy, Protestant. Though men were its primary defenders, Spiritualism was dominated by women. Mediums were mostly female. A medium's power was more than political; the ghosts made her practically divine. (Divine and also wealthy. Mary Andrews earned $1,000 a week in her séance heyday; her husband was happy to encourage her.) Spiritualism spoke to America's so-called enlightened, in other words, those in charge of America's public conscience. These leaders of mid-19th century America had become uncomfortable. They were as restless as the ghosts. They knew that America was getting ready to explode, that she must change ruthlessly and hard. They saw ghosts in their palaces and government halls, in their churches and in their homes. The ghosts were catching up with them, they were America's conscience erupting. When Mary Todd Lincoln moved into the White House she said she saw ghosts everywhere.

She set up a room in the Presidential home for séances just a year before the Civil War's start and the transformation of the country was sealed.

By the end of the Civil War in 1865, half of Americans were ghosts, and Spiritualism went mainstream. Then, just like that, the ghosts were gone. Some of them showed up in England, a few decades later, at the end of the first World War. But in America they silently receded back under the floorboards. In the 1880s, the Fox sisters told the papers that they made the whole thing up. Only nobody would believe them.

Western New York is quiet now. In the Cayuga-Owasco Lakes Historical Society, Moravia's resident historian and one of its last remaining Spiritualists sits in her office cheerfully drawing pies on the backs of fundraiser mailings. Her museum is a single darkish room dedicated to Moravia's most prominent citizen, Millard Fillmore, the accidental president, whose life is showcased with dusty family memorabilia and miscellaneous local items thrown in for filler. In a corner of the room, blocked off by dividers next to the kitchen, is a little exhibit of Xeroxed pictures and newspaper articles providing a short history of Spiritualism. The ghosts are sleeping now, the exhibit says, but they could stir at any moment.

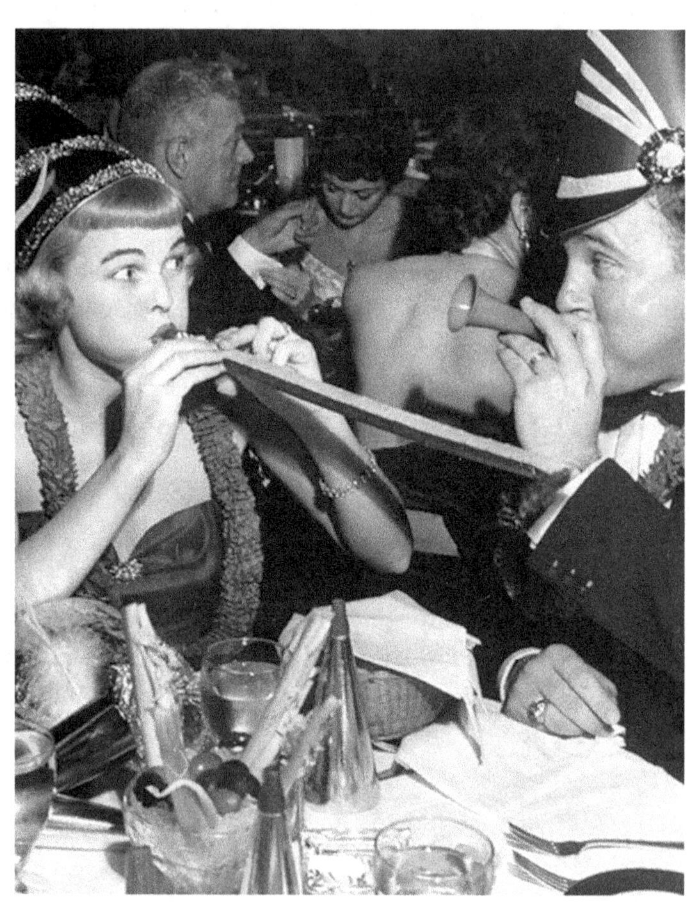

New Year's Eve Pary, 1952

Happy New Year

I woke up late on January 1st. Everything was as it was. I understood then that nothing happens on New Year's and nothing ever would.

The great haiku artist Kobayashi Issa wrote this:

New Year's Day–
everything is in blossom!
I feel about average.

***

Part of New Year's difficulty is that we can't decide if we ought to be mourning or celebrating, if we ought to be dancing in a ballroom or a cemetery.

When the poet Sylvia Plath wrote *New Year on Dartmoor* in December of 1961 and the beginning of 1962 she was herself mostly dead. New year in Dartmoor was to be Plath's last year on Earth, ending in February 1963, when she would quietly put her head in the gas oven and go forever to sleep. In the poem, the speaker walks out to the fresh white snow with her child. She is more ghost than mother, estranged from her child's delight:

This is newness: every little tawdry
Obstacle glass-wrapped and peculiar,
Glinting and clinking in a saint's falsetto. Only you
Don't know what to make of the sudden slippiness,
The blind, white, awful, inaccessible slant.
There's no getting up it by the words you know.
No getting up by elephant or wheel or shoe.
We have only come to look. You are too new
To want the world in a glass hat.

Plath was world-weary in 1962. For the world-weary, newness is a landscape of disorienting, inaccessible slants viewed from far away. The New Year, with its promise of joy and renewal, was a stranger to Sylvia Plath by the time 1962 rang in. She was dying—newness, for Plath, was a lie. Nothing in the world could ever be new to Plath again. Later that year, Plath would give an interview to the British Council and tell Peter Orr that she had a growing interest in history. "I think that as I age I am becoming more and more historical," said the 29-year-old. And so she was, a living artifact before thirty, a ruin who was still able to give interviews.

Here I must slip around and fall over the alien New Year with its mincing falsetto and tawdry gifts, Sylvia Plath wrote to herself. But not even an elephant could bring her back to the magic. Not even a brand-new year. Not even her children.

***

Some people focus on the passing Old Year rather than

the New—English people, for instance, who are nostalgic by nature, as opposed to, say, American people, who do not enjoy the past as much because they have got so little of it, and erase what they do have as soon as they can. "Tread softly and speak low," wrote the English poet Alfred Tennyson in *The Death of the Old Year*, "for the old year lies a-dying."

Old year you must not die;
You came to us so readily,
You lived with us so steadily,
Old year you shall not die. …

He lieth still: he doth not move:
He will not see the dawn of day.
He hath no other life above.
He gave me a friend and a true truelove
And the New-year will take 'em away.

Grieving for the Old Year is the real celebration for Tennyson, who was at his poetic best in grief. The Old Year is adored as a dying king whose rule was, all in all, pretty good. Whatever troubles the passing year brought, there was, at least, some laughter and friendship and love. Good-old comfortable Old Year! Who knows what the New Year will bring? The uncertainty of the New Year's reign-to-be makes the Old Year's reign benevolent by default. "The cricket chirps: the light burns low: 'Tis nearly twelve o'clock." The Old Year grows thinner and colder, the Old Year is almost a shadow.

Step from the corpse, and let him in
That standeth there alone,
And waiteth at the door.

There's a new foot on the floor, my friend,
And a new face at the door, my friend,
A new face at the door.

Tennyson's poem reminds us how the excitement of renewal is always tempered by the sadness of loss. "Step from the corpse, and let him in," wrote Tennyson. But who was the real corpse? What is the passing Old Year or was it Tennyson himself, making way for the Tennyson-to-be? No wonder New Year's resolutions are so fraught—when we invite change into ourselves we die a little bit too. And yet, to deny the New Year altogether, as Plath wished to, is to die completely.

***

Something in us wants to be reborn—otherwise, why mark time? I don't believe that clocks are simply the offspring of the marketplace, a way for civilization to synchronize its achievements. Each new year, each new day, each new minute we are asking for a chance to start over. And we *are* starting over – over and over – so often we can't feel it happening. A part of us does not want to feel it happening, of course, because each passing second reminds us (if unconsciously) of death. The renewal of New Year's is exciting until we remember we are one step closer to oblivion.

Maybe we are asking too much of ourselves. To reflect back upon a whole year gone? To plan for a whole year ahead? So Long to the Past and Hello to the Future? Trying to mentally sum up the entirety of one's life and reaffirm it all on one drunken holiday? It's no wonder New Year's is depressing.

And yet, something remarkable does happen on New

Year's. It can't be denied. It doesn't happen in the Old Year or the New, on New Year's evening or day. But there is a New Year's moment. I don't know how long it is but I know how it feels. The New Year's moment is a gasp, a fracture, a tiny quiet Apocalypse. It happens in that transient middle space between what was and what will be; it is a standing-at-the-threshold-between-the-old-king-and-the-new-face-at-the-door. It is disorienting—Plath saw this. At the New Year's moment, the two years face each other as mirrors, each spanning backward and forward infinitely, so that we can't tell which is which. We don't even know when the moment comes—it might not even be at midnight. A moment can't be planned because it comes too quickly; a moment can't be reflected on for just the same reason. A moment is of time and outside of time because it simply must be lived. This moment is the thing we want to hold on to when we get excited about New Year's, but it is so unpredictable. We get caught up wondering how we will be changed by this moment, and what it will mean. But maybe the possessive 's' after the words "New Year" was put there to remind us yet again how time is not our own. All we can do is open the door between the Old Year and the New Year and invite the moment to arrive.

"This is newness," a poet once wrote while walking with her child through the snow.

the sudden slippiness,
The blind, white, awful, inaccessible slant.
There's no getting up it by the words you know.
No getting up by elephant or wheel or shoe.
We have only come to look.

Plath, in her profound and profoundly sad way, had

found the words for something beautiful as she was trying to find the words for her pain. She had discovered the words for the New Year's moment. The New Year's moment is a sudden slippiness, an inaccessible slant. We can't get to newness by elephant or wheel or shoe, but anyway, we have only come to look.

***

The poet Kobayashi Issa suffered greatly in his life – suffered as we all, in time, suffer – and like us, Issa's suffering informed his opinions about New Year's. Beginning with his mother at age three, Issa's loved ones seemed always to die—his grandmother, his children, his wife. No one Issa loved was immune. Issa's body of work is a chronicle of loneliness and loss. It is not easy to laugh when everything in life goes wrong. Which is what makes Issa's reputation as a funny poet even more significant. For example:

fallen among
the moonflowers …
horse turds

Issa was also a Buddhist and so had a Buddhist perspective on New Year's. He was inclined to view the big through the lens of the microscopic. (Issa wrote no less than 200 poems about frogs, around 230 on the firefly, over 150 about mosquitoes, 90 on flies, and over 100 on fleas, not to mention his gentle meditations on excrement and flatulence.) Issa began his autobiographical work *The Spring of My Life* with a New Year's story. It went like this. Long ago, in Fuko Temple, there was a devout priest who was determined to celebrate New Year's to the fullest. So on New Year's Eve he wrote a letter to himself and asked a novice to deliver the letter back to himself—the priest—in the morning. On New Year's Day, the novice entered the priest's room and handed him the letter. The priest quickly opened the letter and read aloud. "Give up the world of suffering! Come to the Pure Land. I will meet you along the way with a host of bodhisattvas!" And then the priest began weeping so hard the tears soaked his sleeves.

This story is weird, wrote Issa. Who would want to celebrate New Year's in sleeves soaked with self-induced tears? And yet, wrote Issa, what better way to celebrate New Year's?

> Still clothed in the dust of this suffering world, I celebrate the first day in my own way. And yet I am like the priest, for I too shun trite popular seasonal congratulations. … The customary New Year pine will not stand beside my door. I won't even sweep my dusty house, living as I do in a tiny hermitage constantly threatening to collapse under harsh north winds. I leave it all to the Buddha, as in the ancient story.

The way ahead may be dangerous, steep as snowy trails winding through high mountains. Nevertheless I welcome the New Year just as I am.

And then the poet wrote,

New Year's Day–
everything is in blossom!
I feel about average.

Issa's words are not a complaint after all. Letting oneself feel average at the break of the New Year is another way of saying, I accept this year just as it is and myself, just as I am. Can it be that the wild, miraculous sensation of newness comes at the moment when we aren't doing anything?

Welcoming renewal 'just as I am' seems to be a paradox. The New Year is not ours to change, but we can become changed by it. Another translation of this same poem by Sam Hamill goes:

New Year greeting-time:
I feel about average
welcoming my spring.

Issa's standing 'as he is' before the wonder of the Buddha and Time and Nature (*everything is in blossom!*) reminds me of Caspar David Friedrich's painting *Woman before the Rising Sun*. I should like to re-title the painting New Year's Moment. A woman in a long dark dress stands facing a sunrise that bursts up from behind a mountain. The rays of sun blaze and illuminate the rocky landscape, turning the sky a fiery orange. The woman is quite far from the sunrise but Friedrich positioned her in such a way that the rays seem to be shooting out of her whole body. And even so, she is not contorted in ecstasy before the new day. She's not grasping at the sunrise either, trying to gather the sun into herself. She simply stands there, waiting, her arms turned slightly open. This painting is sometimes called *Woman before the Setting Sun*. Caspar David Friedrich—who was not a Buddhist (but was German)—often mixed up time in his paintings. Now something is rising, now something is passing, now something is dying, now something reborn—nature and time always infinite, and mysterious, happenings to stand before in mute awe. Friedrich once said of his paintings (meaning, his life), "I shall leave it to time to show what will come of it: a brilliant butterfly or maggot." This is exactly what the woman in *Woman before the Rising Sun / Woman before the Setting Sun* is doing. She opens her hands a little bit toward to the coming sun and invites the new day to arrive. She welcomes her spring as the winter passes, leaving time to show what will come of it.

(Translations of Issa by: Robert Hass, David G. Lanoue and Sam Hamill.)

Internet Photo (unattributed)

Waiting

Meditations on waiting come in cycles. We've always waited—to live is to wait. It's a devastating thought. To live is to wait.

We haven't always known we're waiting. For millions of years, we waited to evolve, we waited for ourselves, but we didn't know we were waiting then. For millions of years after that, as animals, creatures of the land, we waited in the way that animals do. We waited for seasons so that we could eat, we waited for birth so that we had purpose. But still, we didn't know that we were waiting. So we weren't actually waiting. We were just being. And then, at some point, long ago but not so long ago that we cannot remember, we started to have consciousness, awareness. We learned that we could control the things we waited for, could plant what we most desired to eat, and so forth. And with this understanding, we stopped just being and started waiting.

The last time we really considered waiting may have been the 1950s and 1960s, when Existentialism was popular. Existentialism put thinking about waiting back on the menu, because it was primarily a philosophy that sought to understand Time and what we were supposed to do about it, this airy abstract concept that affected every little thing we did yet had no control over.

In 1953, the world saw the first production of the play *Waiting for Godot*. The plot of *Godot*, if one can call it that, a plot, is this: two men distract themselves while waiting (for Godot) with a variety of amusements including but not excluding: telling stories, eating, singing, sleeping, exchanging hats, talking about the past, hugging, thinking about leaving, and contemplating suicide. The men are named Vladimir and Estragon and the play is in two acts. In 1956, Irish literary critic Vivian Mercier wrote that, with *Waiting for Godot*, Beckett had "achieved a theoretical impossibility—a play in which nothing happens, that yet keeps audiences glued to their seats. What's more, since the second act is a subtly different reprise of the first, he has written a play in which nothing happens, twice." Because Godot never arrives, no one has ever been sure what to believe about Godot, about what or who a Godot is. Some people think that Godot really does show up, though the details of this are mysterious. A lot of people interpret Godot as Death, that Vladimir and Estragon spend the play waiting for death, and thus, that the act of waiting is like dying. But waiting is more insidious than that. Waiting is not dying; it is absence. In the act of waiting, we spend a whole bunch of energy trying to fill up all the absence, but as we do so, everything just keeps feeling emptier. Still, it doesn't stop us from trying.

Because *Waiting for Godot* is not about Godot but about waiting, thinking about Godot leads us into the very same trap that Vladimir and Estragon fell into, i.e. that if you just think hard enough about waiting you can start to live again. Beckett was fully aware of the emptying out of life that happens when you are thinking about waiting. And when he himself started thinking about waiting, he had an insight into a terrible truth: Never again, Beckett knew, can we wait and just be. Now, when we wait, we are inevitably thinking about waiting—the two are inextricable. Waiting had become consciousness of Time, horrible oppressive Time. Time is God. What we are doing when we are waiting/thinking about waiting, Beckett told us, is trying to get closer to God. Meaning just this: When we wait, we are trying to control the uncontrollable, to understand the incomprehensible.

***

On a platform, a woman stares down the tracks, looking for the face of a train. She is wearing red, maybe to attract the train, to pull it closer to her, faster to her, like the woman of Babylon in Revelations hastening the end of the world with her clothes. There is a man too, several men, they are looking at their wrists, shifting around, trying to act casual, trying to hold it together. The platform is full of men and women, waiting, waiting to get home—or to go… somewhere? Each of them is listening to a private concert—presumably, understandably, different private concerts, though one wonders what would happen if all the musics could suddenly be heard at once. It would be a fitting soundtrack for the chaos of waiting.

How is waiting for an arrival different than waiting for a departure? Is there much of a difference, really, between coming and going?

Just this year, an American man named Harold Camping

figured out that the end of the world was happening, that Judgment Day was nigh, and that it would happen on May 21, 2011. He figured out this date with numerology. As they waited, Camping and his followers occupied themselves by advertising for Judgment Day. All around the country, billboards were put up and announcements made on the radio. Campings' believers passed out flyers on the street and invested their life savings into the campaign. Why not? Many quit their jobs to prepare for the looming end times.

On May 21, 2011, Judgment Day did not come. At least, not in the form that was recognizable as such, and so if Judgment Day did come it didn't count. But even Harold Camping admitted that no Judgment Day had come. He had been mistaken, Camping told his followers, told the press. May 21 was not Judgment Day. All the same, Camping then said, the end of the world was still happening. On October 21, 2011, just like he had predicted.

What did all these believers do when the wait was finally over, when no Judgment Day came? Of course, we know. But this question is irrelevant anyway. What makes us understand the world the way we do, what shapes us, is not that events will happen, but that we wait for them to happen.

***

WHAT WE DO WHILE WAITING

1. Look at the time. (note: we can't control time!)
2. Look at each other.
3. Look at books.
4. Look at billboards and flyers.
4. Look at devices that play music.

5. Think about our day past.
6. Think about the day ahead.
7. Think about waiting.

***

We all focus our lives around some BIG EVENT, or intermittent series of big events, with an endless smorgasbord of activities thrown in. Dates are the markers of these events. Dates and times. Calendars and clocks don't tell us what we do. They tell us what we wait for.

Waiting has become one of the more difficult tasks humanity faces. With each new tool we make to count Time, speed Time, slow Time, waiting becomes more and more terrible. The most difficult thing about waiting is, as we agreed, being forced to have a relationship with the unknown. Technologies have gotten better at helping us predict the future, with the result that our waiting time —i.e. our time spent in the presence of the unknown—is minimized. But it's still not enough. It's never enough.

Is waiting a state of being or is it an act of consciousness? It's hard to say. One thing we know, though. Waiting is undesirable, regrettable, at times frustrating as all hell, and to be avoided at any cost. Waiting signals a breakdown of order. In modern times, when we are waiting, it's because we think that something is not functioning properly, someone isn't doing their job.

This might be my own hang-up, but lines are the worst form of waiting after the ultimate wait—waiting for death —which is to say that waiting in lines is the worst occasion of waiting after life itself. I once wrote a song that compared standing in lines to little deaths, drops into the infinite when you feel that your very self has no reason, no power, when you think about the past and future at once, and it takes everything you have to maintain an atmosphere of order and sense. In other words, to maintain patience. Often, when we are waiting together, the patient are considered weak. The strong rail against waiting. You can tell who are the strong ones in a waiting situation. How dare you make me wait? is something they might say. But let's not forget that patience is order, and impatience is chaos.

I called the song 'Queuing Theory'. Queuing theory is the study of waiting in lines. Examples of Queuing theory occasions for study are:

– waiting to pay in the supermarket
– waiting for information
– planes waiting to circle before they can land
– waiting to be served in a restaurant
– waiting for a train

About waiting, you might ask:

– what is the average waiting time of a customer?
– how many customers are waiting on average?
– how long is the average service time?
– what is the chance that one of the servers has nothing to do?

Queuing theory is useful for people in operations management, for helping businesses get the most bang out of their waiting buck. It helps businesses decide just how much or how little control they can or need to have over their customers' waiting times. If you are a mathematician, knowledge of Queuing theory might make you more or less patient in a waiting situation. But mathematicians know the disturbing fact about Queuing theory. They know that the models for Queuing theory often assume infinite numbers of customers, infinite numbers of 'queue capacity'. Queuing theory often predicts wait times for a world that has no limit to waiting. Some think this is a flaw of the theory. But perhaps it is a secret truth, a secret we all know, too.

***

By allowing ourselves to wait we are making one very presumptuous presumption about life: that we actually have somewhere to go, something to do. Waiting pisses us off, but without waiting, how would we know if our lives had meaning?

Waiting makes us angry, too, because of all these expectations that we have about Time, but the reason we have expectations is that we expect Time to move in a linear fashion. Time has a beginning and an end. Anyone who tries to suggest otherwise, that time perhaps moves in circles or spirals or, like the String Theorists, that there are multiple times existing concurrently—these people are duly denounced and ignored. Time, as we ALL KNOW, has a beginning and it has an end. When we step on to the train platform, we are starting one moment—the imminent arrival of the train—that we know will end with a final act—the arrival of the train. When the train doesn't come, we don't just get annoyed, we get scared. We are terrified when the train doesn't come because it's at this moment that we start to think to ourselves: Maybe I've got this wrong. Maybe there is no ending, and no beginning either. Maybe my whole life is an infinite loop of this: getting to the train, getting on the train, being on the train, leaving the train, missing the train, never having gotten on the train. But if that's the case, then my life is continuity. If that's the case, I don't have to ask, "What am I waiting for?" If that's the case, I'm never really waiting. I'm never waiting for time to pass, because for time to pass it has to eventually start and stop. If that's the case, maybe waiting is just another word for living. It's a devastating thought though, I would say. To live is to wait. To live is to wait.

***

There's a sigh of relief when the train finally comes, but why? It's not as though lives have changed by this fact, the train's arrival, even one tiny bit. But it feels like it. The end of a wait feels like a movement towards something. The end of a wait feels like the beginning of something new. But if you can live inside the waiting, can be present for the wait, rather than wishing it finished, rather than holding your breath, you can almost trick yourself into believing that you are really living.

Stefany Anne Golberg

Joesph Roth, Paris, mid-1930s

A Life in Letters

Among the 457 letters in *Joseph Roth: A Life In Letters*, there is not one love letter. This may not surprise fans of the writer—author of *The Radetsky March*, *The Emperor's Tomb*, and *Job* among others—who may know Joseph Roth as a vagabond and misanthrope whose occupation as a journalist had him traveling from one European country to the next, living in rented rooms, wearing threadbare clothes, without a bank account, mostly alone, too miserable for romance, the consummate Wandering Jew. But even Roth the World War I soldier left no love letters, no tender requests to, perhaps, a girl he left behind in the crumbling Hapsburg Empire, asking for solace or maybe a photo. Nor did he write any romantic epistles to the lovers with whom he found companionship and comfort in his final years.

There are a handful letters from Roth's prewar younger days, but they are all written to his cousins in Lemberg. They are letters of encouragement, advice, pontificating, the kind of letters one writes in youth that are more an affirmation of one's self-understanding: "I am a sworn enemy to etiquette," he wrote to his cousin Resia (which, in any case, was not true) and "…just like in Goethe's Faust, which, alas and alack, you haven't read." "Who ever would have guessed it: all of nineteen!" he wrote to his younger cousin Paula when he was twenty-two. "But then nineteen years are like a piece of fluff on the scales of eternity. And it's in eternity that we live. From eternity, in eternity, for eternity. Yes, *for* eternity as well."

There are no love letters—or any letters at all—to his wife Friedl Reichler, from whom he was often separated for long stretches between travels. There was a time when Roth had Friedl in tow, a lifeline to the world outside the mobile office of his hotel rooms, to the world outside his mind. But even when, in 1929, Friedl's unhappiness turned to insanity—when she was eventually shipped back to her parents, and then, finally, committed to an asylum (where she would be "euthanized" by the Nazis in 1940) leaving Roth desperately, achingly free—he only wrote letters to his in-laws, hurried inquiries about Friedl's health, and whether his payments to doctors had been received. The letters were cordial and encouraging but brief, to the effect of: I'm hoping the book will be sold soon, I'm trying to get more money, please don't take Friedl's aggression personally, not sure when I can visit but soon. The last ten years of Roth's life were dominated by work, alcohol, and the guilt-ridden struggle to keep Friedl financially, if not emotionally, provided for.

Almost none of Joseph's Roth's surviving letters are what one might expect, or hope, to see in a book subtitled "A Life In Letters". As editor and translator Michael Hofmann aptly notes in his Introduction, there are no letters written by Joseph Roth to his parents. Roth never knew his father, who lost his mind before Roth was born and died in Russia when Roth was sixteen. There are no letters to his mother, whom Roth barely saw, but he never fails, in his correspondences, to inquire after other people's mothers (and other people's wives). There are no letters written to those who, according to Hofmann, were perhaps Roth's closest friends—even after Europe became a continent of exiles in 1933 and a letter from a friend would be a critical comfort.

The letters of Joseph Roth are at once intimate and distant, impersonal and revelatory, candid and somehow incomplete. Most letters are written with a characteristic Joseph Roth formality, but this makes for striking contrast with the furious passion of the content. There is rarely self-censorship with Roth and yet the blunt frankness often feels more like a show than honesty. "Sorry, forgive the know-it-all tone, the superiority, and anything else that bothers you here. Listen, if you do listen, to the *absolute honesty* of my words," he wrote to a fellow writer Hans Natonek in 1932. As Hofmann discovered in translation, Roth rarely used the familiar *Du* (in the original German) and when he did it was for, as Hofmann puts it, "near-strangers", fellow soldiers with whom he had briefly served in the Austrian army, and only then because it was dictated by custom. Even when Roth was informal it was because the rules of formality called for it. For instance, his letters to friend, patron, and fellow writer Stefan Zweig, with whom he had a friendship that spanned over a decade in multiple countries, and to whom the majority of his later letters in *A Life In Letters* are addressed, begin with "Dear Esteemed Mr. Zweig" and sometimes "Dear and Esteemed Mr. Zweig," and once as "Dear highly esteemed Stefan Zweig." This formality was adhered to even when Roth was asking Zweig for money or expressing his fears ("I am terribly sad…my wife was my only channel to the world outside, the social part of myself. My own glumness scares me."). Soon after they first met, Roth begins a letter to Zweig with, "I must yield to your wish that I not address you as "Mr." if you think it impedes the friendliness of our communications. That it honors me, I need not say," addressing the letter to the "esteemed Stefan Zweig." No doubt, Stefan Zweig was esteemed; not only was he older and far wealthier than Roth, but among the most famous European writers of his day. Nonetheless, Zweig's admiration for Roth was obvious in Zweig's lasting patronage and friendship, which continued faithfully—despite Roth's notorious and ever-increasing cynicism—until Roth's suicide at the age of forty-four in 1939.

Prior to 1929, the majority of Roth's correspondences were with his protégé Bernard von Brentano and boss Benno Reifenberg, men with whom Roth had both personal and professional relationships. While the tone of these letters is familiar, the professional aspect of his relationship to them never disappeared. In fact, he seems to use his correspondence with these men as an arena for the perpetual battle between Roth and World. With the younger Brentano, who replaced Roth (with the latter's help) as Berlin correspondent at the *Frankfurter Zeitung*, Roth uses a patronizingly paternal and self-obsessed tone not unlike the one he used with his little cousins. He is alternately critical and supportive of Brentano, never without a word of advice. A sympathy letter Roth wrote to Brentano in 1927 is telling:

> Dear friend, the news of your father's death just reached me.... I never got to meet him, but even so I mourn his passing. I imagine he was one of those characters that no longer exist in Germany, a person with the aura of the Counter-Reformation, and the Holy Roman Empire....

> I mourn his death of course not least for you, my friend, because you still needed him, and it would have been only fair if he had lived to see your literary fledgling....
>
> Don't take it amiss if I tell you that such moments are necessary and even fruitful. They attach us to the beyond, it's a little like going to church, which of course we don't do.... Write to me through Miss Weber—but only if you want to....

And in a 1929 letter to Pierre Bertaux (the son of critic Félix Bertaux, another friend cum associate) Roth writes of Brentano, "He is one of the three or four people I would happily murder, with no more compunction than putting out a cigarette."

The tension between personal and professional is most profound in his letters to Benno Reifenberg, Roth's boss and editor at the *Frankfurter Zeitung*, where Roth was a star journalist. There is a warmth in Roth's letters to Reifenberg—Roth is always sure to give his best to Reifenberg's wife and son—and Roth is comfortable sharing his sorrow with Reifenberg as well as his pleasure. Note one of his first letters to Reifenberg from Paris, where Roth served as correspondent for the *FZ* in 1925, doubtless the happiest year of his life.

> I feel driven to inform you *personally* that Paris is the capital of the world and that you must come here....

(Ironically, Reifenberg would come to Paris, and eventually become Paris correspondent himself for the *FZ*.)

> I owe it to you that I was able to come to France, and I shall never thank you enough.... My wife is staying here for the moment, she's unwell.... Please write to her.

But the letters never escape the characteristically strained relationship between difficult writer and amiably aloof editor. Roth is forever plaguing Reifenberg with requests for more money, or for praise, or for confirmation of the publication of his work, or simply confirmation of Roth's existence in a return letter. Reifenberg continued to be patient and helpful, but it was never quite satisfying for Roth.

The fact that these people, like Zweig, continued their relationship with Roth, bearing the constant criticisms which came attired sometimes in white gloves, sometimes in vitriol, is both a testament to their devotion and to their position in Roth's life as intimates he could keep at arm's length. Reading his letters, one gets a sense of Joseph Roth's power. He had a way of making people feel utterly esteemed or utterly worthless, depending on his mood or on their behavior toward him on any given day. Perhaps Roth used "honesty" as much to distance himself from the world as to bring himself into it. It's almost as if Roth wrote letters to express his deepest torments to the people for whom it would matter the least. Over and over, Roth begged his colleagues for correspondence, was desolate when none came, yet never stopped trying to prove to others how much relationships were an imposition upon his solitude. "Never have I cared less about people," he wrote to Zweig in 1930. "Never did they seem more intrusive and less inclined to leave me alone. And they can't have given much for what happened to me."

The tightrope Roth balanced between formality and informality was also a delicate balancing of past and present. Born in 1894 in the Galicia of the Austro-Hungarian Empire, Roth was witness to the collapse of an entire world, the world of European empire that gave way to the world of modern European nation states. He was a monarchist who couldn't believe in the promises of nationalism; a Jew in an anti-Semitic society (who later considered himself a Catholic); an Austrian whose postwar home was in Germany, a country he lived in only periodically; a German writer who worshipped France, whose city of birth turned Polish and then Ukrainian, who had no father, whose wife was insane, who lived out of three suitcases, who didn't even own a copy of any of his books; a man of the East and the West, the past and present, but never the future. "I am never at home," he wrote in 1933 to Félix Bertaux, "just wander around randomly, I can't stand to be in a room."

Forever homeless, Roth was nostalgic for a life that he never really knew, that never even really existed. But this was beside the point. The old world of Joseph Roth was a world of order and sense, of standards, of stability. "If only the traditional forms still applied!" he wrote once to Brentano. "But the new informality in Germany kills everything. I can't participate." This sensible old world, or the old world as it existed in his longing, is what Roth – an artist naturally disposed to internal chaos living in a chaotic world, where barbarians had taken over and a Hell reigned on Earth—craved. The characters in the thirteen novels Joseph Roth pushed out of his brain in less than twenty years all grapple with some version of this theme: How to return to a place and time that exists only in the imagination. How to feel at home.

Why read a book of letters written by a writer of books? Letters are the opposite of a book. A book is careful, constructed, thoughtful; letters are messy and immediate and can be insultingly thoughtless. It is the combination of all these things that makes the letters of Joseph Roth so moving, and disturbing, to read, especially as a companion to his novels. There is melancholy in Roth's novels, but the melancholy is tempered with joy. There was nothing tempered in Joseph Roth's letters, and there was no joy, not in his letters nor, it seems, his life, save his early days in Paris. "I have become an old man," he wrote at the age of 36, "and have gotten used to the absence of joy. In my own life, that is." Sometimes Roth's letters read like sketches for future novels, an excising of his own worst psychoses, psychoses that he wouldn't dare inflict upon his closest friends and family, the people who depended most on his better qualities—his generosity, his sensitivity—or on the fictional characters he created in his novels, the characters that recur in his books like old friends. Perhaps Roth saved up all his joy for his characters. Or maybe he lived joyously through them.

Giving up on the possibility of finding a home in the world, Roth devoted his life to escaping his own internal homelessness through two means, alcohol and writing, and it is unknown which killed him first. Ironically, he would die in the only country that ever gave him pleasure, France, a country where the exuberant ease he so admired was as foreign to him as the German stuffiness he hated.

Emily Dickinson once said something about letters reminding her of immortality because they are "the mind alone without corporeal friend." The letters of Joseph Roth are the documentation of a mind alone without corporeal friend in a breathless race toward death. It's like what Roth wrote to his cousin long ago: "It's in eternity that we live. From eternity, in eternity, for eternity. Yes, *for* eternity as well." One gets a glimpse of the man who has come to be a literary spokesperson for nostalgia, but in Joseph Roth's letters, nostalgia's darker side is revealed. It is a nostalgia that has no room for a life lived today, nostalgia as a timeless, placeless dream that can never be, a dream without room for the dreamer.

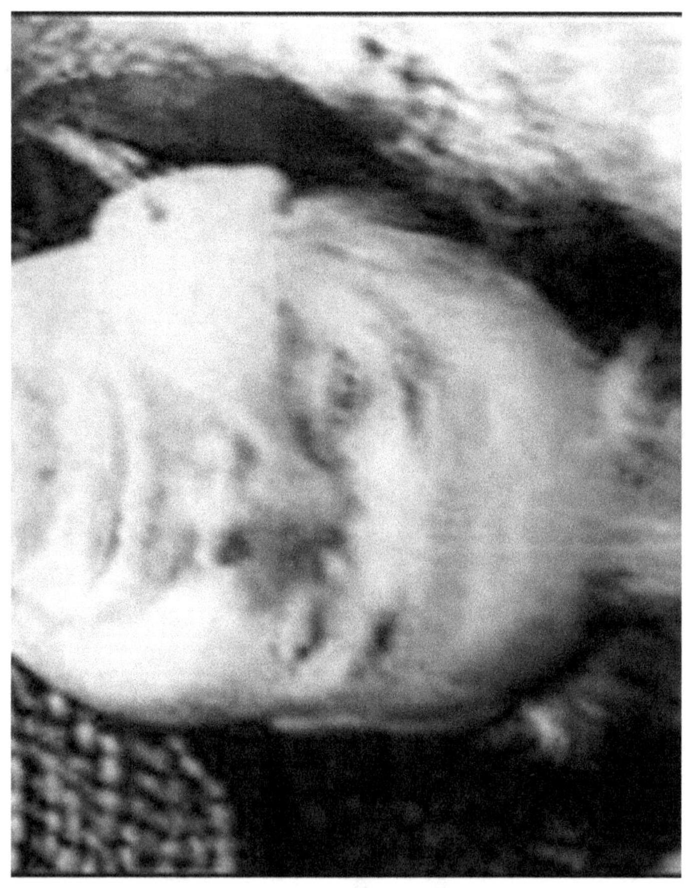

Photograph provided by the Romanian Government showing Nicolae Ceausescu moments after his execution, 1989.

Kings

They dug up the body of Nicolae Ceausescu. Or did they? It was Christmas Day 1989 when the Romanian dictator (along with his wife Elena) was executed. But there are those who still won't believe it. So on July 21 of this year, 2010, Romania dug up the body in Ceausescu's grave, to perform DNA tests on it, and to pronounce Nicolae Ceausescu dead, once and for all.

In "The Great Christmas Killing," Hungarian author Peter Nadas wrote about the Ceausescus' execution as he saw it on television ten years after the fact. He describes in stark detail the scenes before the killing and after, from the hasty trial to the hurried postmortem examination. "The captors of the dreaded Ceausescu couple…forced them into a space between the wall and the two steel-legged tables. Either it was cold in the room, or the uniformed members of the summary tribunal did not permit the tyrant and his wife to take off their coats." He writes of the moment when the hands of the Ceausescus are tied behind their backs with clothesline as they protest, indignant, and the terror of the attending physician whose entire body shakes as he is called on to show the camera, the world, that Nicolae and Elena Ceausescu are gone.

Conspicuously absent from Nadas' account is the killing

itself, which happened too fast to be captured on tape. Participants later explained that, as the couple were led outside to be shot, the captain of the execution platoon got an itchy trigger finger, and fired first before giving the orders. Once shots were heard everyone started blasting like gangbusters. They seemed desperate to get the whole terrifying business finished before someone lost his nerve. Watching the film, you can indeed see the scene cut as the couple is led outside. By the time the camera is turned back on, guns are firing, but the Ceausescus are already dead. The actual shooting of the dictators, the moment when bullet hits flesh, is undocumented. Since there is no recorded proof of the killing, some Romanians have declared, who can say they were shot at all? Perhaps, they say, an execution did take place, only it was not the Ceausescus whose bloody corpses we saw but body doubles brought in for the show. It's the body doubles, they say, that really lie in the Ceausescus' graves.

Even seeing an execution take place is no guarantee that it will be believed. The killing of Sadaam Hussein, for instance, shakily documented by a guard with a low-res cell phone camera, can be viewed by anyone with a proper internet connection, from beginning to end. You can watch the noose being slipped almost gently over the dictator's head, hear the neck crack, stare into the close-up of his lifeless, gaping eyes. And yet, as in the case of Ceausescu, there are still those who believe that the man in the noose is a look-a-like, that the real Sadaam Hussein walks among us.

It's no easy task to kill a dictator. Partly this is because they have a special kind of life. A double life. In 1957 Ernst Kantorowicz published a classic study on the medieval theory of the rights of kings, which he called "The King's

Two Bodies". Every king has two bodies, he explained, the body politic and the body natural. The body natural is a physical body—a screaming, farting and dying body, just like yours and mine. Knowing that this natural body will eventually die, the king also has another body, the body politic that is the symbol of his divine right to rule. Being divine, the body politic transcends the physical body, allowing for a continuity of the kingdom even when the king had died. In other words, the king's rule is still wielded over his subjects, even after death. As such, a king never really dies. The king is dead, long live the king.

It is really, then, the king's subjects who keep the kingdom (and the king) alive. They are the believers, the ones who have the immortality of the regime woven into their souls. So what happens to the king's subjects when the unimaginable happens, when the kingdoms themselves fall (as in the cases of Iraq or Romania) but its subjects live on? How are they to piece together the disconnected parts of themselves that are neither present nor past? How do you decide what is really dead and what is still alive?

One strategy is to start digging up graves. This need not always be a literal affair. In the halls of the National Council for the Study of the Securitate Archives are files containing information about thousands of Romanian citizens, information that remained hidden from them for years. The archive is itself like a graveyard, containing the past lives of the subjects of the old regime. The Romanian Securitate took great liberty with these lives, constructing the narrative as they saw fit. Few of us can imagine what it must feel like to know your government is rewriting your autobiography, and that you are powerless to influence its contents. To read such a file must be akin to experiencing schizophrenia.

Little by little, the old files of the Securitate (the secret service of the Communist regime in Romania) are becoming available to the public. The Romanian-born German author Herta Müller (winner of the 2009 Nobel Prize for Literature) has been trying to gain access to her own file ever since Communist Romania fell. Last year, twenty years after the death of Ceausescu, she was finally granted permission and wrote about the experience of reading it in an essay called "Securitate in all but name" (*Sign and Sight*, 2009). She learned that the Securitate opened a file on her in 1983, in response to the publication of her first novel *Nadirs*, for "tendentious distortions of realities in the country." Notably missing from the file are records from three years during which Müller was persecuted for refusing to spy for the Securitate. Confusingly, she finds her file not under the name "Herta Müller". Rather, it is called "Cristina".

> In my file I am two different people. One is called "Cristina", who is being fought as an enemy of the state. To compromise this "Cristina" the falsification workshop of Branch "D" (disinformation) fabricated a doppelganger from all those ingredients that would harm me the most – party-faithful communist, unscrupulous agent. Wherever I went, I had to live with this doppelganger. It was not only sent after me wherever I went, it also hurried ahead. Even though I have always and from the start, written only against the dictatorship, the doppelganger still continues on its own way. It has taken on a life of its own.

In dictatorships, you see, the "kingdom" doesn't just

grant two bodies to its leaders. It also creates a second body for its citizens. Or as Müller puts it, a doppelganger. There is the identity created by the self, and the identity created by the State. As far as the State is concerned, Müller and her doppelganger are one. It sounds quite sinister, and it is. Yet all the more devastating is that, for the individuals living under a dictatorship, the bodies can become internally confused. You start to wonder yourself, "Who is the real me? Is there a real me beyond the Party me?" If you read the above quote carefully, you realize that "Cristina", enemy of the State, is not even Müller herself. It is a fictionalized Müller. Meaning, in the eyes of the Securitate, there isn't Müller and her doppelganger. There are two fictional versions of Müller. Müller herself is erased completely.

You might think that when the Wall fell, when the kingdoms died, when the citizens of the former Soviet states were "free", all the extra bodies would have disappeared. You might think that political freedom would have killed the doppelgangers. But just as the king never really dies because his political legacy lives on, the kingdom lives on too through the doppelgangers. This is what Müller means when she writes that the doppelganger continues on its way, takes on a life of its own. After the Wall fell, millions of people were left with a pre-dictatorship self and a post-dictatorship self, both living side by side, in mutual suspicion of the other.

In "Securitate in all but name" Müller wrote, "You can even get used to death threats. They are part and parcel of this one life we have. You can defy anxiety to the depths of your soul. But slander steals your soul." When Müller declined to be a spy, the Securitate simply convinced the people around her that she was one anyway. In doing so, she became the object of mistrust, of hatred. At work, people shouted, "Informer", and she was soon fired. "I was being slandered by precisely the people that I was protecting by refusing to spy on them," Müller wrote. At least if she had been a spy and had been exposed, Müller could have experienced a feeling of punishment for an actual offense against her fellow citizens. Instead, she was punished for what her doppelganger did, which means, what no one did. Müller was forced to endure hours and hours of interrogation where she was asked about her doppelganger's seditious activities. She found herself trying to account for an identity she didn't even know. She was accused of strange trivialities, like sleeping with men for makeup and tights, and told that she would be shown proof of her actions. Such an experience could drive a more fragile person mad. Certainly, it creates an enduring madness in a society, a fragmentation that can never completely be repaired until the last of the regime's subjects have died. Perhaps not even then.

It is the life's work of writers like Müller and Nadas to scratch at the tombs of uncomfortable truths, to come to terms with the doppelgangers by meeting them head-on. They know it is lonely work, that most would prefer to leave their past political selves behind simply by forgetting they ever existed. Müller and Nadas know, however, that such selves are too powerful to die of their own accord. Partly, Nadas explains, it is because the subjects and the king both carry within them the logic of dictatorship. In "The Great Christmas Killing" Nadas quickly admits the absurdity of the Ceausescu's clumsy pre-execution trial. Still, he finds himself dispassionately enjoying the film, as did so many other victims of Eastern Bloc tyranny.

> Being vaguely aware that there had to be something to object to in this outrageously unlawful, dilettante farce—though I had no objection—and that there should be another law-abiding and humane person within me to protest my moral indifference and oppose my aesthetic naiveté—though there was no such person to be found—created a strange vacuum.

Watching the Ceausescu execution, Nadas goes looking for that humane and law-abiding person within himself —the one who ought to protest—and comes up with a vacuum. This empty space is the gap between self and doppelganger, between then and now.

There is no easy path toward filling up that empty space. It means finding and reabsorbing, somehow, the doppelganger out there causing trouble. The problem is that those in Romania who dug up the Ceausescus are looking for the wrong bodies. The DNA tests on Nicolae Ceausescu may very well prove that the body in Nicolae Ceausescu's grave is the physical body of Nicolae Ceausescu. Few doubt that they will. But all the DNA tests in the world can't kill the little Ceausescu that lives inside every Romanian who lived under his rule. The little doppelganger that makes them doubt themselves without always knowing why, that makes them wary of neighbors and think of friends as potential enemies. The "body politic" that makes them feel absent when they are present, present when they are absent. That makes them go digging around in search of bodies when they know the digging will only produce more ghosts. As the body of King Ceausescu is finally pronounced dead, many of his subjects will never fully believe in his death because his real life and legacy live on. "Even though the dictatorship has been dead for 20 years," Müller wrote, "the doppelganger is still wandering about. For how much longer?"

The king is dead, long live the king.

Internet Photo, Daily Mirror, U.K.

Apocalypse

Harold Camping expected a spectacular death. He thought he would see horses and towering flames. Instead Harold Camping fell down at home last month at the age of 92 and never got up again.

Judgment Day is upon us, the radio evangelist proclaimed a few years ago, setting May 21, 2011 as the date. All across America, billboards became Camping advertisements for Apocalypse. "Cry mightily unto GOD for HIS Mercy" was one suggestion, "Joy to the World" claimed another. All across the nation, there were Americans who laughed, and those who readied themselves. Camping's believers stopped paying their credit cards, quit their jobs, said farewell to friends. Some spent their life's savings in preparation for the End—some spent it on the Rapture campaign itself.

When Judgment Day did not come, Camping tried to assuage believers. "Please forgive me, America!" a new billboard read. "I was terribly wrong about … May 21, 2011. There is forgiveness in those who trust in Jesus Christ." Then he said that he had gotten the timing wrong and that the End would, in fact, happen in October. But October passed the same as ever and then Harold Camping had a stroke. By that time, accounts of thousands who had mistakenly given up their Earthly existence came pouring through the news. "Yet though we were wrong," wrote Camping in a letter to his Family Radio Family, "God is still using the May 21 warning in a very mighty way." Look at the millions and billions of people who heard the message of Christ's imminent return, Harold Camping wrote. And, Camping assured us, he would still come.

Reporters and Average Joes expressed outrage at Camping's Rapture campaign. Camping's followers were treated in the media as ridiculous and occasionally as tragic, Camping as a fraud and a heretic. The whole thing is an anomaly, the American media told the world, America is not like this.

But America is like this, and it always has been.

America is a nation rooted in Apocalypse. The very foundation of the nation is tied to the End Times. Apocalypse is in America's DNA. When the Puritans stepped out into the bitter wilds of New England they brought with them the forecast of annihilation. These exiles came to America not to delight in religious freedom but to ring in the last of days. "The Judge draws nigh, exalted high upon a lofty Throne," wrote Puritan poet Michael Wigglesworth.

Amidst the throng of Angels strong,
lo, Israel's Holy One!
The excellence of whose presence
and awful Majesty,
Amazeth Nature, and every Creature,
doth more than terrify. …
Before his Throne a Trump is blown,
Proclaiming th' Day of Doom:
Forthwith he cries, Ye Dead arise,

and unto Judgment come.
No sooner said, but 'tis obey'd;
Sepulchers open'd are:
Dead Bodies all rise at his call,
and's mighty power declare.

In the mid-19th century, William Miller's obscure Millennialist movement became a national campaign. His prophecy that Christ would return to Earth around 1843 or 1844 came to be known as the Great Disappointment. Some of Miller's followers went to live with the Shakers (who didn't need to wait for the new Millennium as they believed it had already come) and the rest formed an entirely new religion and called themselves Adventists. David Berg told us the End would come in 1973 and Pat Robertson guaranteed that 1982 would bring "a judgment on the world". Reverend Bill Maupin from Tuscon, Arizona preached of a rapture that would happen on June 28, 1981. Fifty Arizonians gathered at Maupin's house to be "spirited aloft like helium balloons."

There is one thing that unites all of these Apocalyptic Americans. They do not see America as a place to create a new civilization. They see America as a place to settle into a wilderness of the soul.

***

In 1693, Magister Johannes Kelpius got on a boat to the New World. Kelpius was not going to America to make a new life for himself. He was going to watch life end.

The young Transylvanian was just 22. Behind him, Kelpius left a comfortable life of academic excellence and a prominent clerical family. With him, Kelpius took a profound faith and a small band of fellow believers. Johannes Kelpius boarded in London and headed to the new Province of Pennsylvania across the sea. In his *Diarium*, Johannes Kelpius recorded details of the journey. Like most ocean voyages back then, the experience was hell: lost anchors, devouring winds, a battle with a French vessel.

Upon the open seas, Johannes Kelpius thought about home, and about exile. Earlier that year, the young scholar had fallen under the spell of Johann Jacob Zimmerman, a prominent astronomer and scholar. Zimmerman had lost his position as Lutheran minister in 1685 due to his habit of criticizing the state church and, moreover, his insistence that the Apocalypse would occur in the autumn of 1694. His radical Chapter of Perfection sect read sacred scripture alongside works of astrology and numerology, the Kabbalah and the writings of Jakob Böhme, a German shoemaker and mystic. After working out the numbers, Zimmerman thought that America—in particular the city of Philadelphia, a sparsely settled refuge at the edge of the forest—would be the best place to experience the Apocalypse. Indeed, the whole American project seemed to Zimmerman a practical invitation to the End Times. In the secluded woods surrounding Philadelphia, Zimmerman's Pietists would live in celibate simplicity, anxiously waiting for "that happy day," wrote follower Johann Gottfried Seelig:

> which when its new Earth swallows all that forementioned Floud and where its glorious Sun causeth all other Stars and Phoenomena to disappear, no Night succeeds it, but that the Night is swallowed up in ye Day, Darkness into Light, Death into Life, Judgment into Victory, Justice into Mercy, all imperfect Metals into Gold, and Gold itself is refined seven

> times, and all Churches and Virgins comprised into the one Dove .... the Sons of God will shout for joy as they did in the Beginning, when God was all in all, as he will be all in all, when again the Earth hath found its beginning.

In the New World these Philadelphia mystics would become known alternately as The Hermits of the Wissahickon, The Hermits of the Ridge, The Mystic Brotherhood, The Society of the Woman in the Wilderness.

Just before they were about to set sail from Rotterdam, Johann Jacob Zimmerman died, leaving Johannes Kelpius leader of the Society. Johannes Kelpius gathered his followers about him and said goodbye to his European home forever. A few weeks later, floating between future and past, Kelpius quoted a passage from Seneca in his diary:

> I cannot go beyond my country; it is the one of all; no one can be banished outside of this. My country is not forbidden to me, but only a locality. Into whatever land I come, I come into my own: none is exile, but only another country. My country is wherever it is well; for if one is wise he is a traveler; if foolish an exile. The great principle of virtue is, as he said, a mind gradually trained first to barter visible and transitory things, that it may afterwards be able to give them up. He is delicate to whom his country is sweet; but he is strong to whom every single thing is his country; indeed he is perfect to whom the world is exile.

Johannes Kelpius was never looking for a home in America; he was looking to make himself homeless in the world, and in doing so, ready himself for heaven.

***

We are taught that America began as a home for exiles—but what does that really mean? The words "home" and 'exile" are as seemingly opposed as two words could be. For Johannes Kelpius, those coming to America to make it into their home were missing the point. Kelpius saw America as temporary and transitory, a mere pit stop between the world and eternity.

Kelpius' Apocalyptic approach to life does not seem conducive to building monuments or governments or making sure credit card debts are paid. And yet, it is interesting to note that the first mission of Kelpius and his monks when they came to Philadelphia was to build a Hermitage of stone. Though they intended to live there in solitude, the monks—respected scholars in Europe with training in medicine, science and music—found their lives immediately entangled with the small community of settlers around them. In the great hall of the Hermitage, they held public nondenominational religious services twice a day. The monks built a schoolhouse for the children of settlers and were consulted for medicinal cures. They offered all of their services for free and refused to trade for profit. In the evenings, the Monks of the Wissahickon would meditate and look through the telescope they had erected on the roof of the Hermitage. They followed the stars and waited patiently for all their efforts to be destroyed.

The impulse behind the building of Johannes Kelpius' Hermitage is the same impulse that compelled Camping's Family Radio to spend one hundred million dollars on billboards. Both are temporary monuments that hold inside them the tension between Earthly works and oblivion. That tension is always present for Americans who live life in the shadow of the Apocalypse, reminiscent of something the poet Issa once wrote, that the world is a world of dew "and yet, and yet… .". No matter how developed America gets, for Apocalypticists she will always be a wilderness.

www.ingramcontent.com/pod-product-compliance
Lightning Source LLC
Chambersburg PA
CBHW060151130626
46556CB00006B/2587
* 9 7 8 0 6 9 2 4 2 7 8 3 5 *

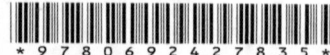